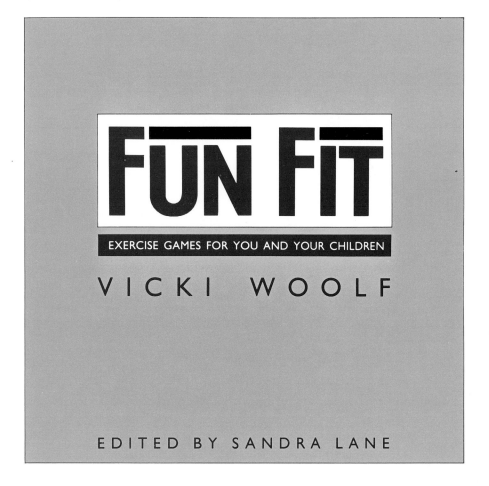

FUN FIT

EXERCISE GAMES FOR YOU AND YOUR CHILDREN

VICKI WOOLF

EDITED BY SANDRA LANE

Conran Octopus

FUN FIT

This book is for David Belcher, Bronwen's dad and my husband, with our love

I have a confession to make – I had a co-author on this book, my eight-year-old daughter Bronwen. Together we devised and named these exercise games, and tried them out with Bronwen's friends Sophie Smith, Risa Tabastnick and Joanna Haldane. We would like to thank Karen and Stephen Wood-Ward, Thomas Khoolas and Chloe Diski for all their hard work and perseverance in helping demonstrate the exercises at the photographic sessions. I would also like to thank their mums, my friends Sue Wood-Ward, Maddy Khoolas and Jenny Diski, for letting me borrow them. My thanks also to Bonnie and Tony Tabastnik for their friendship, Tim Woodcock and Mike Davis for allowing us to turn their studio into a playroom, and to Patrick Butler for his constant help and support. Lastly, my loving gratitude to my own mother, Basila Sieff, for looking after Bronwen while I was writing this book . . . . VICKI WOOLF

This edition published 1986 by
Conran Octopus Limited 28-32 Shelton Street London WC2 9PH

ISBN 0 85029 027 X

Art editor: **Ann Burnham**
Design: **Grundy & Northedge**
Illustrator: **Coral Mula**
Photographic references: **Tim Woodcock**

The publishers would like to thank Christine Hill, M.C.S.P., S.R.P. for her assistance with checking the exercises, and Elisabeth Morse for checking the nutritional sections.

Typeset by Text Filmsetters Limited, London. Printed and bound in Hong Kong

CONTENTS

ARMS AND CHEST

WAIST

LEGS

BOTTOMS

HANDS AND FEET

YOGA

FUNFIT combines exercise with play in a way which I hope you and your family will enjoy. I devised the exercise games over the last two years with the help of my eight-year-old daughter Bronwen, to keep her happy and amused.

As a mother I realised how easy it is to become unfit when you are housebound with small children to look after and haven't the time or opportunity to take exercise. And the same goes for the children; they need lots of exercise to grow supple and strong, develop good balance and co-ordination and build up self confidence.

But nowadays, most of us drive everywhere or take buses rather than walk. Many families live cooped up in flats without gardens to run about in, and television, our main source of entertainment, lures us away from more active pastimes. This lack of exercise is thought to be the main reason why in Britain our weight is slowly rising – even though our food intake is falling.

So it is up to us to keep our bodies running smoothly and keep them strong and healthy by taking exercise. However, the exercise one can take in the home is limited, and repetitive exercise routines quickly become boring – especially for children.

So I wrote *Fun Fit* to solve the problem. I tried each exercise with Bronwen in order to find the perfect combination: exercises that give your muscles the best workout and you the most fun.

There are times when all mothers are plagued with cries of 'Mum, I'm bored . . .'. This is where *Fun Fit* comes into its own. When Bronwen is bored I take out the book and we play some of the games together. She quickly forgets about her boredom and enjoys herself, and at the end of quite a short session we both feel relaxed and refreshed and Bronwen is ready to continue playing on her own.

A wonderful side-effect of exercise is that it can actually change your mood for the better. The stresses involved in coping with demanding children produce an adrenalin build-up which can make you snap, slap, and then feel guilty. Exercise helps to burn off the adrenalin and with it irritability, which is why just a half-hour session can leave you feeling so refreshed. So get moving!

EATING FOR HEALTH

As well as taking enough exercise, to be really healthy you must eat well, too. And, today, experts agree that most of us eat too much fat, sugar and salt and too little fibre. Eating well can improve our chances of living a long and healthy life. A few years back the government set up a committee to look into the links between what we eat and modern diseases. The results of this research showed that there were strong links between heart disease and obesity and eating too much fat. Too much sugar in the diet can cause tooth decay and encourage obesity, and in some people a high salt intake can lead to high blood pressure and strokes. But it was found that eating lots of fibre can help prevent bowel disorders, as well as play a useful role in keeping weight down, as fibre-rich foods are both filling and often low in calories. And keeping weight down, reduces the risks of heart disease and strokes.

Less fat, sugar, salt and more fibre. It should be simple, but when it comes to putting these new guidelines into practice most of us come unstuck. But it really is quite easy, isn't more expensive or time consuming and doesn't mean shopping at health food shops, especially as many supermarket chains are producing foods that are low in salt and sugar. Look for them when you go shopping. Be more aware of what you are eating and always check the labels of the foods you buy to see just what goes into them – you'll be surprised.

It can be hard to change the eating habits of a lifetime, but here are some simple ways to make the changes that even the fussiest eaters in your family shouldn't object to.

FAT

Fat is our number one enemy. Weight for weight fat is twice as fattening as carbohydrates such as pasta, bread or potatoes. Fat makes up about 40% of the calories we consume – too much. Most of it is found in meat and meat products, cooking and spreading fats and dairy products such as milk and cheese. Too much fat can push up cholesterol levels in the blood which can lead to heart attacks in later life. One in three of all men in Great Britain will be affected or even killed by heart disease before they retire. Aim to cut fat consumption by about a quarter, ideally things you find easiest to do without.

Cut down by
● Eating less meat. Eat only the lean cuts of meat and cut away any fat you can see before cooking. Eat more white meats such as chicken and turkey. They contain less fat (especially if you discard the skin as well) and they're cheaper. Cook more fish instead of meat.
● Grilling or baking meat and fish (or fish fingers).
● Spreading butter or margarine more thinly.
● Cooking a little meat in casseroles with lots of vegetables.

Choosing cheeses such as Edam, Camembert and Brie which contain much less fat than Cheddar, Stilton or Cream cheeses.

Changing to skimmed milk. If you find the change too great mix skimmed milk with whole milk, and gradually increase the amount of skimmed milk as you find it more acceptable.

Eating chips less often. Either make them at home, cutting them thick and straight (crinkle-cut chips absorb more fat) or try the oven-baked varieties which contain the least fat.

Starting the day with a cereal instead of a fried breakfast.

Avoiding shop-bought meat pies as they contain high amounts of fat to make the meat go further and to prolong shelf life.

SUGAR

Sugar is full of empty calories that help make us fat and harm our teeth. Brown sugar and honey are just as bad as refined white sugar and we could do without all of them since we can get all the sugar we need from healthier sources such as fruit. Sweets are often given as a reward or to show affection which heightens their attraction for us as we associate them with pleasant feelings. So never reward your children with sweets. They are safest eaten at the end of a meal: it is sweet foods and drinks eaten *between* meals which do most damage to teeth. Half of the sugar we eat comes added to foods such as cakes, biscuits and drinks and it even turns up in ketchups, soups and sauces.

Cut down by

not eating sweet things between meals. Nibble instead on pumpkin or sunflower seeds, fruit or raw vegetables. See page 126.

Avoiding sugary, fizzy drinks. Look instead for low calorie squashes or unsweetened fruit juices and add fizziness by diluting them with fizzy mineral water or soda water.

Diluting unsweetened fruit juices.

Serving fresh fruit for pudding sometimes.

Buying supermarket brands of muesli that contain no sugar; add sweetness in the form of fresh or dried fruit.

Tread carefully with children, it pays to reduce sweetness slowly by:

Mixing sweetened fruit yogurts with natural yogurts or natural yoghurt with unsweetened fruit purée.

Mixing the sweetened version of a breakfast cereal together with the unsweetened version.

Always check food labels for sugar content; sometimes sugar is called glucose or sucrose. The higher up the label it appears the higher the proportion of sugar present.

SALT

We eat an average of two teaspoons of salt per person a day. Much of it comes added to the foods we buy, so look for 'no salt added' labels. Aim to cut your salt intake by about a quarter.

Cut down by

Eating less of smoked or cured meats such as bacon, ham, salami and salt beef.

Avoiding salty snacks such as crisps.

Replacing salty snacks with roasted pumpkin or sunflower seeds, nuts and raisins or breadsticks.

Adding lemon juice instead of salt when cooking vegetables.

Not putting salt on the table when you are eating.

Seasoning food with more herbs and spices, or lemon juice.

FIBRE

Fibre is the name for carbohydrates found in the cell walls of plants – often called roughage.

To eat more fibre

Eat plenty of fresh fruit and vegetables.

Eat fruit and vegetables with their skins on whenever possible.

Choose wholegrain foods such as wholemeal bread and pasta, brown rice and wholemeal flour.

Used rolled oats (porridge) for crunchy toppings instead of traditional crumble.

Include more brown rice, potatoes, vegetables and pulses in your main meals.

Snack on dried fruit, nuts and raw fruit and vegetables.

Aim to eat something high in fibre at each meal. (List of high fibre foods below).

HIGH FIBRE FOODS

Try to include one of the following in each meal:

beans, like baked beans; sweetcorn; wholegrain cereals; wholemeal bread; brown rice; potatoes in their skins; vegetables such as cabbage, leeks, spinach, turnips, spring greens, peas and green beans; fruit such as apples, bananas, oranges, blackberries and raspberries; dried fruit; nuts.

BUT WHAT ABOUT VITAMINS?

You might be wondering whether you'll be getting enough vitamins by following these guidelines, but you needn't worry. Providing you

7

eat a good variety of foods – including plenty of fresh fruit and vegetables – your vitamin intake should be adequate.

Make sure your food is high in vitamins by buying only the freshest fruit and vegetables and cooking your vegetables for as short a time as possible: always eat them in their skins.

Vitamins begin to escape from vegetables and fruit soon after they are cut into, and into cooking water. So don't cut them up too small and either steam or cook them in a tiny amount of water (no need to cover the vegetables with water) and keep the water to use in soups and sauces.

Carefully frozen vegetables are a good second best to really fresh vegetables. Frozen peas actually reach us in better condition than those you can usually buy in greengrocers as the picking, packing and cooking process is so efficient that it preserves the maximum amount of vitamins.

IN BETWEEN MEALS . . . .
For healthy snack ideas for staving off pangs of hunger in between meals, turn to page 126 where you'll also find suggestions for well-balanced, tasty and nutritious packed lunches for all the family that have been devised by a leading nutritionist.
Note: Babies have special needs and you should consult your health visitor or doctor before altering their diet.

PLAYTIME
The exercise games can be played at any time during the day except just after a heavy meal. Working muscles need a good supply of blood, so the stomach will be deprived and therefore unable to digest your food properly.

Do the more active games when your child is most bouncy and lively, and the more gentle restful ones closer to bedtime to calm him/her down. However, the cool-down exercises, which come at the end of the book and should be done after every bout of exercise games, will help to encourage relaxation and sleep.

PLAYWEAR
Do the exercise games barefoot, but make sure there aren't tiny pieces of Lego lying around to tread on. Wear loose cotton clothes (cotton tracksuits are ideal) that are easy to move in, keep muscles warm and allow sweat to evaporate. Women should wear a comfortable bra for support.

PLAYROOM
The games should be played in a room that is sufficiently large and free of furniture or breakable things to avoid accidents. The temperature should be comfortably warm and the room well ventilated. Remove slippery rugs from bare boards – fitted carpets are best to exercise on. Play the exercise games in the open air if you can but not in very hot or very cold weather when your body will be using most of its enegy to adapt to the temperature.

BREATHING
Some people – particularly children – are inclined to hold their breath when exercising or holding a difficult position. Breathing in is usually no problem, they just forget to let it go.

Good breathing like good posture enables you to exercise your body to the best of its ability. To breathe properly you must stand correctly. A slumped body compresses the ribcage and the diaphragm which makes for shallow breathing. Hold up your head and feel first your ribcage expand then, lower down, your tummy as you breathe in deeply, then slowly release the air. Deep, even breathing benefits the heart and lungs and brings gulps of oxygen into the body and into our blood stream to fuel our muscles as we move them.

OUCH CRAMP! WHAT IS IT?
Cramp can be quite frightening, especially for children. The sudden involuntary contraction of a muscle or group of muscles without warning can be very painful. It most commonly strikes legs and feet.

Cramp results from a build up of the waste product of the energy process, lactic acid, which causes muscles to contract. It is most common after strenuous exercise, because the blood cannot wash away the lactic acid quickly enough.

Dancers and athletes frequently get cramp. But sometimes you get cramp when you are asleep because you have a limb in an awkward position, squashing veins that would normally be transporting the lactic acid away. As cramp is caused by muscles over contracting, gently stretching those muscles will relieve the pain. To cure cramp, sit on the floor and bend down to your toes and gently pull them back towards you. If a young child has cramp lie him on his back and raise his leg, hold it straight against your hip and gently press his toes back towards his body. With a bigger child gently lean your body against the foot to flex the toes back.

A WORD OF WARNING

Although all the exercise games in this book have been thoroughly checked for safety by a physiotherapist there are some exercises (these are clearly indicated in the text) that should not be attempted by those with back problems. If you have *any* health problems, however slight, seek your doctor's advice before starting *Fun Fit*. Never exercise during or immediately after an illness, even after a cold and especially following a viral infection; give your body time to regain its strength. Mothers who have had a baby within the last six months shouldn't attempt to play any of the exercise games as some of the ligaments take at least six months to fully recover their strength, and the lower back is particularly vulnerable to strain.

Fun Fit does not outline a lengthy exercise routine, it is meant to be dipped into and enjoyed, so do as many or as few of the exercise games as you feel like doing. Having said that I must stress the importance of always warming up and cooling down. *Never* do any of the exercise games without first warming up your muscles with some

of the gentle stretching exercises in the Warming-Up section: it is when you exercise on cold muscles that strains occur. Cooling down after energetic exercise is just as important. Slow, rhythmic movements take your heart beat and breathing back to normal without placing a strain on your system.

Always remember that exercise should *never, ever*, hurt. And while feeling a little stiffness during the two to three days following exercising is okay – feeling aches and pain, however slight, is not. It means you have pushed yourself too far, too soon, or you haven't warmed up properly before starting the exercise games. Children can get over excited easily and overdo things – so they must be watched carefully.

While each section of *Fun Fit* aims to work different parts of your body such as tummy, bottom, waist or legs, many of the exercises work the surrounding muscles to tone up the whole area and often many other parts of you as well.

To get the best from your body you must use it correctly. Always start an exercise from a position of good posture or you may use the wrong sets of muscles and possibly strain yourself. There are correct ways to bend, sit and lift too. First, learn to stand correctly. Good posture isn't holding your body rigidly straight, but standing in a way that puts as little strain as possible on your muscles, bones and internal organs. Imagine a string pulling from the top of the back of your head and feel it gently pull, lengthen and relax your whole spine starting from the top of your neck. Your shoulders should go down, back and relaxed, shoulder blades flat, not poked out and there should be only a slight curve in the small of the back. Your bottom should be neatly tucked under and your tummy held in. Your knees should be held comfortably straight not rigid and your feet should be slightly apart and point outwards a little. If you encourage your children to stand well from an early age you'll protect them from back problems in later life.

When lifting anything heavy always bend at the *knees* and go down into a squat, keeping your back as straight as possible, then lift the object by straightening your legs again. Legs are well equipped with lots of muscle to do this job. Compare thigh and calf muscles with those on your back, where the muscle is hardly thicker than a rasher of bacon, and obviously not meant to take great strains.

If a member of your family is handicapped in any way they may love to join in some of the exercise games in *Fun Fit*. Show *Fun Fit* to your doctor or physiotherapist to see which ones might be suitable for your child. All physical skills are based on movement and all children – handicapped or not – love using their bodies to find out all about how they work, developing their physical skills to become increasingly strong, deft and agile.

9

INTRODUCTION

Always do some warming-up exercises before attempting any of the exercise games. It is when you suddenly jerk or contract 'cold' muscles that injuries occur. Gentle warming-up exercises slowly stretch your muscles, stirring up the circulation to increase the blood supply to your muscles – literally warming them up – which makes them capable of more vigorous exercise. Warming up wakes up your mind, too, making you feel more mentally alert. Even such fit people as professional dancers and athletes, warm up before training or performing.

The following exercises will gently ease your body into action in preparation for the games to follow. Also, you will find some more warming-up exercises in the Hands and Feet section.

TOUCH THE SKY

FOR ADULTS, AND CHILDREN FROM EIGHTEEN MONTHS.

Aim: warms up, stretches and loosens up the whole body.

Really stretch your body and see who can be the straightest and the tallest. Don't hold your breath while you stretch; breathe deeply and evenly.

I Stand up straight with your feet comfortably apart, tummy in and bottom tucked neatly under. Lift your arms above your head and stretch up towards the ceiling, first with one hand and then the other. Stretch ten times with each hand.

SEMAPHORE

FOR ADULTS, AND CHILDREN FROM EIGHTEEN MONTHS.

Aim: to warm up the body and strengthen shoulder and arm muscles.

Pretend you are sending messages in semaphore. Move your arms briskly and smartly, keeping them as straight as possible – you must signal clearly. Breathe in as you raise your arms, out as you lower them.

1 Stand up straight with your feet comfortably apart, tummy in and bottom tucked neatly under. Stretch your arms out in front of you level with your shoulders.

2 Raise one arm straight up above your head, then return it to the starting position. Do the same with your other arm, then repeat up to twenty times – ten times with each arm.

3 Raise both arms together above your head (make sure to keep them straight). Lower them back to shoulder level and repeat up to ten times.

keep your bottom tucked under

At the Kremlin

FOR ADULTS, AND CHILDREN FROM EIGHTEEN MONTHS.

Aim: to warm up the body.

The soldiers of the Red Army who guard the Kremlin in Moscow have to march like this, stiffly raising their arms and legs in turn. It is called the 'goose step', and probably helps to keep the soldiers warm. It will help you to warm up, too.

1 Goose step in time with a friend across the room, keeping your arms and legs straight and raising your legs as high as possible.

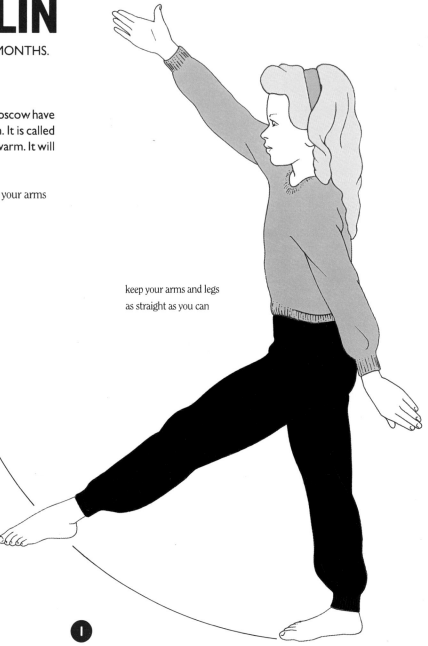

keep your arms and legs
as straight as you can

GRAND OLD DUKE OF YORK

Now be one of the grand old Duke of York's ten thousand men and march briskly across the room, and back again. Remember to stand up as straight as real soldiers.

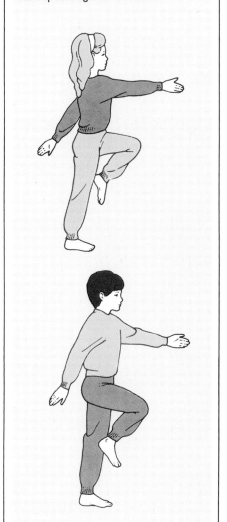

13

WINDMILL

FOR ADULTS, AND CHILDREN FROM EIGHTEEN MONTHS.

Aim: Warms up body and stretches arms, legs, hamstrings and back.

In this exercise move your body like a windmill by bending from the waist to draw big circles with your arms – the windmill sails. The wind blows your sails to help grind the flour.

1 Stand up straight, head up, tummy in, bottom tucked under, feet comfortably apart, and stretch your arms high above your head.

2 With your hands together draw a big circle with your arms. Swing them out sideways and down round towards your right foot, across to your left foot and up in an anticlockwise direction back to the starting position. Repeat up to ten times then stop and circle ten times in the opposite direction.

②

don't force yourself to touch your feet – just go down as far as is comfortable

②

BROKEN WINDMILL

Now pretend that the sails of your windmill are stuck and won't turn a complete circle.

Stand with your feet apart, head up, bottom tucked under, tummy in. Then keeping your back straight, bend from the waist and swing your right arm down towards your left foot, at the same time swinging your left arm back out to the side. Then, without straightening up, swing your left arm across to your right foot. Don't worry if you can't quite touch your feet, just go as far as you can. Repeat fifteen times and gradually work your way up to twenty-five.

15

BIG DIPPER

FOR ADULTS, AND CHILDREN FROM EIGHTEEN MONTHS.

Aim: warms up, stretches and strengthens the whole body, in particular the arms, wrists, back and inner thighs.

The swooping and dipping movements of this exercise are similar to those experienced on board the big dipper at the fairground. The arms imitate the loops, while the body plunges down and rises steeply, just like the real thing. But this exercise won't leave you feeling green.

1 Stand up straight with your feet a little more than hip-distance apart, tummy in and bottom tucked under, and stretch your hands above your head.

2 Winging your arms out sideways bring your hands round down towards your feet as you drop into a deep plié, with your knees apart and your back straight.

3 Slowly bring the palms of your hands up together and rise up out of the squatting position, keeping your back straight.

4 Slowly rise to full height bringing your hands up above your head. Then separate your hands and begin again. Repeat up to twenty times.

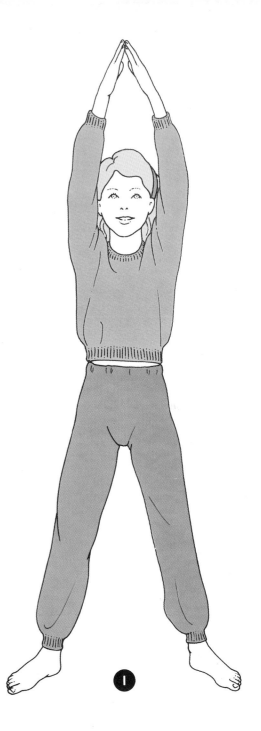

don't poke your bottom out

3

keep your back in a straight line

2

4

17

GRENOUILLE

FOR ADULTS, AND CHILDREN FROM THREE YEARS.

Aim: warms up and stretches the whole body, strengthens leg muscles and helps improve co-ordination in children.

Re-enact the old French pastime of catching frogs to eat for supper.

1 Children should crouch down into a frog-like squat and leap forwards as fast as they can – just like a frog – in order to escape the hungry French person (Mummy) who is creeping up behind them.

land lightly like a frog, not an elephant

1

18

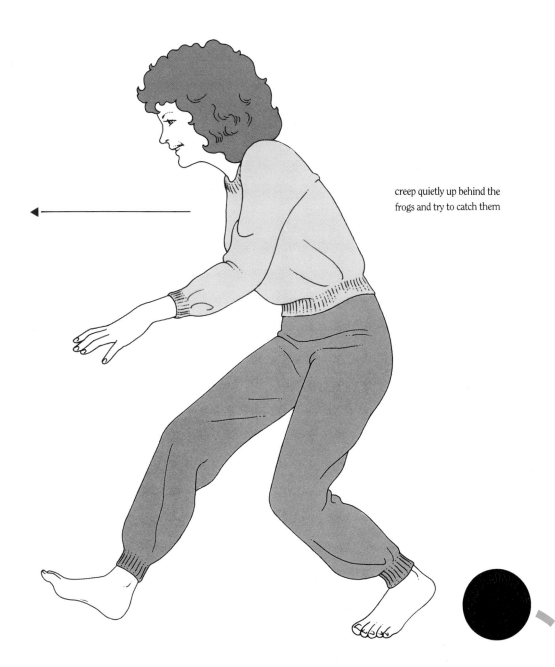

creep quietly up behind the
frogs and try to catch them

JIMINY CRICKETS

FOR ADULTS, AND CHILDREN FROM EIGHTEEN MONTHS.

Aim: warms up shoulder and thigh muscles and strengthens lumbar spine. Encourages physical dexterity and co-ordination in children.

This exercise is similar to those hand-clapping games where it is infuriating when you don't manage to clap in time together. In this exercise you have to clap upside down – see if you can get your timing right.

1 Stand back to back with your partner, a few inches away, with your feet apart and hands and arms stretched above your head.

2 Keeping your back as straight as possible, bend your knees and bend down and slap the floor.

3 Swing your hands under your body through your legs and clap your partner's hands. Repeat ten times, breathing out on each swing down.

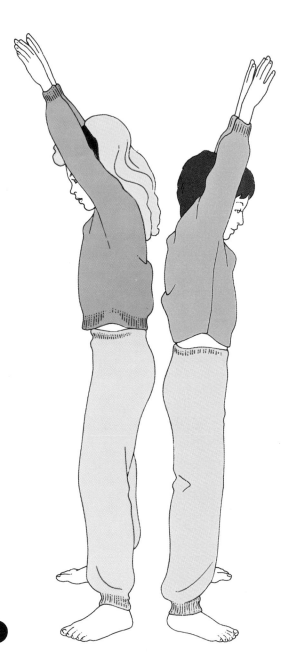

1

keep your bottoms touching
as you clap your hands together

ROCKING CHAIR

FOR ADULTS, AND CHILDREN FROM EIGHTEEN MONTHS.

Aim: warms up body, works arm, shoulder and pectoral muscles, and strengthens hamstrings.

Imitate the gentle rhythm of a rocking chair in this exercise, to give all your main muscle groups a good stretch. But don't let anyone sit on you; this would harm your back.

1 With your feet wide apart, bend your knees and place your hands on the floor sufficiently far away from your feet to enable you to keep your legs comfortably straight. When your weight is taken on your arms, keeping your back straight, straighten your legs.

2 Take your heels off the floor and rise onto the balls of your feet and rock forwards and back again to the floor. Repeat up to ten times, keeping up a slow and steady rhythm.

Then bend your knees, take your weight back onto your legs and, with your back straight, stand up.

1

2

stop the instant your knees start to hurt

RUNABOUT

FOR ADULTS, AND CHILDREN FROM EIGHTEEN MONTHS.

Aim: to loosen up and warm up all over before starting on the exercise games.

1 Play 'he' or 'it' by chasing each other around your house or flat or garden. To prevent a fall, always follow your child up the stairs and go down the stairs in front of him. Put away easily broken things and check there are no slippery rugs or loose stair carpets.

don't run too fast, just a gentle jog

1

23

INTRODUCTION

The following exercises will increase the strength and mobility of your arms, chest and shoulders, and strengthen those muscles that help us to maintain healthy posture.

Tension can set in around the neck and shoulders, sometimes causing stiffness or even headaches. These exercises will help to keep this area supple and relaxed.

Remember to take extra deep breaths when working arms, chest and shoulders to counteract any restriction to breathing caused while working these muscles.

Many women hope that exercise will restore firmness to breasts that have lost some of their elasticity. While exercise cannot restore breasts to their former shape, it will make the most of them whatever their shape, by toning the underlying muscles and the area around the bra strap which can so easily become flabby.

GOALIE

FOR ADULTS, AND CHILDREN FROM EIGHTEEN MONTHS.

Aim: works arm, chest and shoulder muscles, and helps to keep back flexible.

In this exercise you use your body as a human goalpost to trap balls under your chest as they are rolled through. Take it in turns with your child to be goalie or goal shooter.

1 To be goalie, kneel on all fours and keep your back and your arms straight.

2 Lower your back, keeping it straight (don't let it dip in the middle) and, bending your elbows sideways, lower yourself to the floor in a kneeling position (bottom on your heels) until you can touch it with your chin. Then return to the arched position. Now get your goal shooter to roll a ball towards you. As the ball rolls under you, lower your body as described in order to stop the ball and prevent a goal being scored. Then change positions.

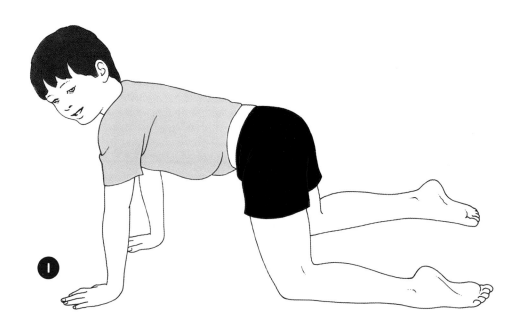

1

score a goal as you trap the ball with your body

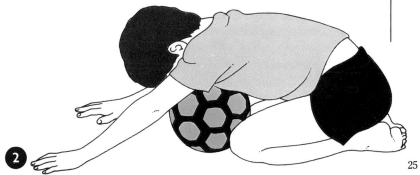

2

ORANGES AND LIMES

FOR ADULTS, AND CHILDREN FROM EIGHTEEN MONTHS.

Aim: strengthens muscles in arms, shoulders and wrists, and stretches back of legs.

This exercise is another version of the game 'oranges and lemons'. But you use your body to trap your victims instead of your hands and arms. Partners must be the same size.

1 Kneel on all fours. Take care to keep your back straight throughout this exercise, don't let it dip or hollow in the middle.

2 Straighten your legs and rise onto your toes to make a large arch for your partner to crawl through.

3 As your partner crawls under your body, try to catch them.

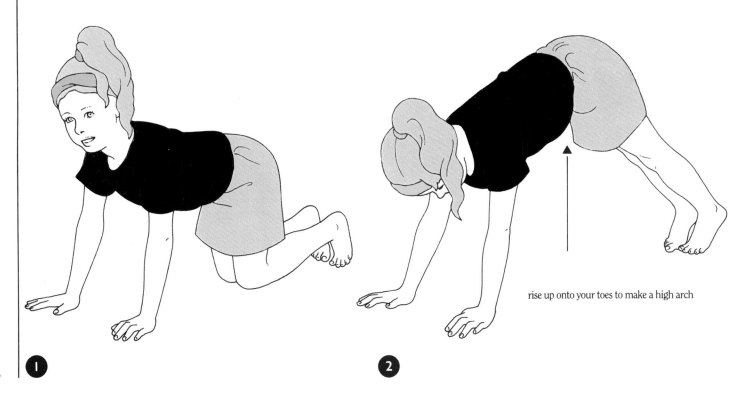

rise up onto your toes to make a high arch

26 | **1** **2**

4 Slowly and carefully lower yourself back into a kneeling position on top of them. Now change places.

Oranges and lemons said the Bells of St Clements,
You owe me five farthings said the bells of St Martins

When will you pay me said the bells of Old Bailey?
When I grow rich said the bells of Shoreditch.

When will that be? said the bells of Stepney.
I do not know said the great bell at Bow.

ARMS AND CHEST

4

3

now get your friend to crawl underneath you

27

LONDON BRIDGE

FOR ADULTS, AND CHILDREN FROM EIGHTEEN MONTHS.

Aim: strengthens muscles in arms, wrists and shoulders, and stretches hamstrings.

London Bridge now lies in the middle of an Arizonan desert where it was moved to in 1968. But this exercise is about the very first London Bridge that burnt down in the great fire of London.

① Kneel on all fours with your back straight and toes tucked under, ready to push yourself up.

② Breathe in deeply, drop your head down and push up onto your toes. Keep your back as straight as possible.

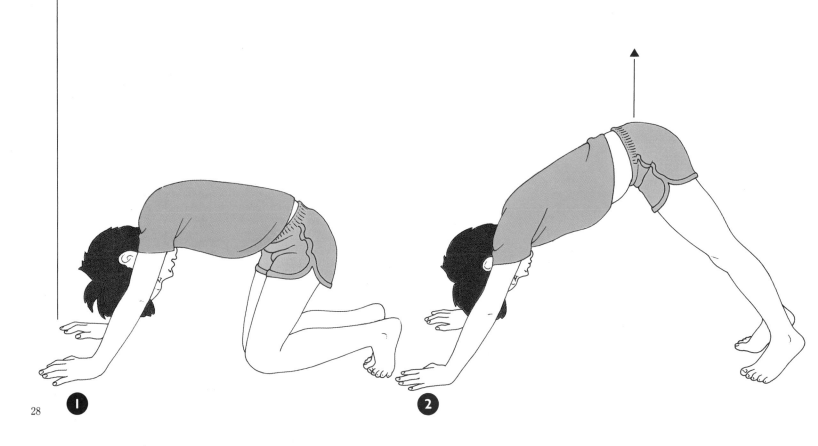

28

3 Push your bottom up as high as you can making a good strong bridge shape, while keeping your legs comfortably straight. London bridge is falling down: gradually, as if in slow motion, drop back down onto your knees, keeping your hands stretched out in front of you.

4 Sit back onto your heels and bring your face to rest on the floor as the whole bridge collapses. Relax in this position for a moment then repeat from the beginning.

London Bridge is falling down, falling down, falling down,
London Bridge is falling down, my fair lady.

Build it up with iron and steel, iron and steel, iron and steel,
Build it up with iron and steel, my fair lady.

Iron and steel will bend and bow, bend and bow, bend and bow,
Iron and steel will bend and bow, my fair lady.

Build it up with gravel and stone, gravel and stone, gravel and stone,
Build it up with gravel and stone, my fair lady.

Gravel and stone will fall away, fall away, fall away,
Gravel and stone will fall away, my fair lady.

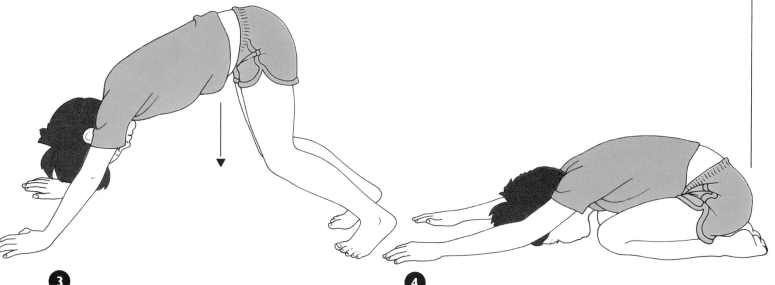

3

4

LADY-LIKE PRESS-UPS

FOR ADULTS, AND CHILDREN FROM FIVE YEARS.

Aim: strengthens arms, shoulders and chest muscles.

This exercise is especially good for toning the pectoral muscles that support the breasts and firming-up flabby upper arms.

1 Lie face down, legs straight and together with your arms bent and hands, palms down, to either side of you.

2 Push your body off the floor until your arms are straight, keep your hands and knees touching the floor, and your back as straight as possible. Slowly and carefully lower your body back to the starting position. Repeat up to four times, breathing in as you rise, and out as you lower yourself.

do *not* attempt this exercise if you have any history of back problems

SCORPION

FOR ADULTS, AND CHILDREN FROM FIVE YEARS.
Don't attempt this exercise if you have any back problems.

Aim: gives the whole body a good stretch (particularly the spine) and strengthens arm and chest muscles.

When the scorpion is in danger he raises his tail and curls it back on himself ready to sting anything that threatens his life. Be a scorpion and bend your body back on itself. Children are often more supple than adults and find this position easier to achieve. Never force yourself into this position, just go as far as you comfortably can.

1 Lie face down, legs straight and together, hands on the floor directly under your shoulders.

2 Push yourself up on your arms as in the previous exercise. Bend your head back, and bend your knees and point your toes back towards your head as far as is comfortable. Breathe in and out again as you slowly relax back to the starting position.

3 As you become more supple you can attempt to touch your head with your toes. But don't let anyone 'help' by pushing your toes and head closer together; this could harm your back.

INTRODUCTION

The waist is one of the most difficult parts of the body to exercise effectively. Many people push their bottoms out and stand badly, thus exercising the wrong parts of themselves and possibly straining their back muscles. It is very important to start an exercise from a position of good posture – and that doesn't mean stiff 'army' posture: shoulders wrenched back and head poked out. In fact, in order to stand well your spine should be lengthened and relaxed. Start at your head. The back of your neck should be straight, not curved with your chin jutting out. Your shoulders should be down, back and relaxed, shoulder blades shouldn't poke out, your back should barely curve. Hold your tummy in to prevent pelvic tilt, and too much hollowing of the small of your back. Legs should be gently flexed at the knee, not rigidly straight, feet should face forwards or be very slightly turned out.

Finally, to work your waist muscles well when stretching from side to side, try to keep your pelvis as still as possible and, if you're standing, don't move your feet.

BELLY DANCER

FOR ADULTS, AND CHILDREN FROM EIGHTEEN MONTHS.

Aim: tones and works the waist, thigh and tummy muscles.

Imagine you have a huge wobbly belly (they are much admired in Turkey!) and do a belly dance. Undulate your hips by moving your pelvis round in big circles – hypnotize your audience with your skills.

1 Stand straight but relaxed with legs comfortably apart, knees slightly bent. Rotate your hips in a voluptuous fashion, circling ten times to the right, then ten times to the left. See who can writhe the best.

THE TRIANGLE STRETCH

FOR ADULTS, AND CHILDREN FROM EIGHTEEN MONTHS.

Aim: tones, works and strengthens back and waist muscles.

To help maintain correct posture and work your waist muscles effectively, try doing the exercise standing with your back against a wall.

1 Stand up as straight as you can, tummy in, bottom tucked under, feet wide apart, hands by your sides.

2 Bend over to the right as far as you can (without cheating by leaning slightly backwards or forwards) and slide your right hand down the right side of your body, while bringing your left hand and arm up into a bent position on your left side. Then push down again a little bit further to the right. Now do the same to the left. Repeat twenty times.

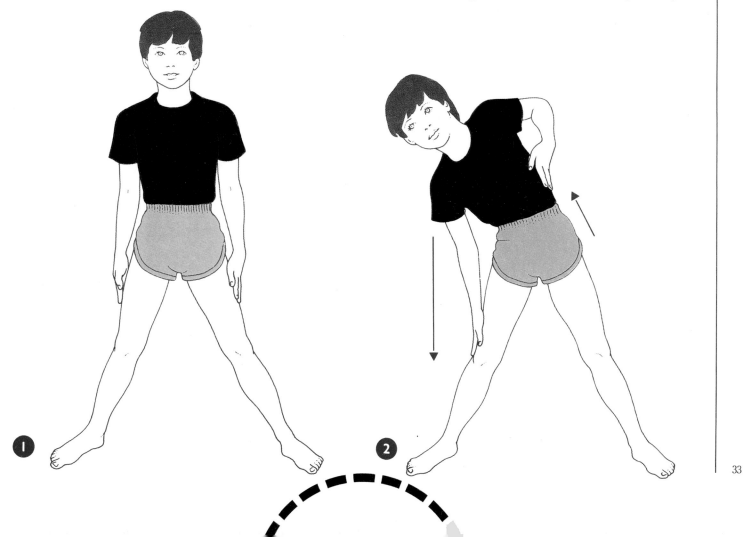

33

TRIANGLE FLOOR STRETCH

FOR ADULTS, AND CHILDREN FROM EIGHTEEN MONTHS.

Aim: gives a healthy stretch to waist, inner thighs and hamstrings.

Do this exercise with someone close to your own size. Sit back to back and synchronize your movements well and you'll make a lovely star shape.

Take care not to strain knees or thigh muscles by forcing your legs too wide apart.

1 Sit on the floor with your back straight and spread your legs as wide as is comfortable. To help you sit straight, pretend you are a puppet with a string attached to your head that pulls you gently upright. If you feel your partner slump, tell him to pull his strings up!

1

2 Bend over sideways to your right, swinging your left hand over your head and pushing down with your right hand to touch your right foot. Don't worry if you can't reach it, just go as far as you can. As you and your partner are sitting back to back, your partner will have to bend to his left and touch his left foot. Push down ten times, keeping your legs straight. Repeat to the other side.

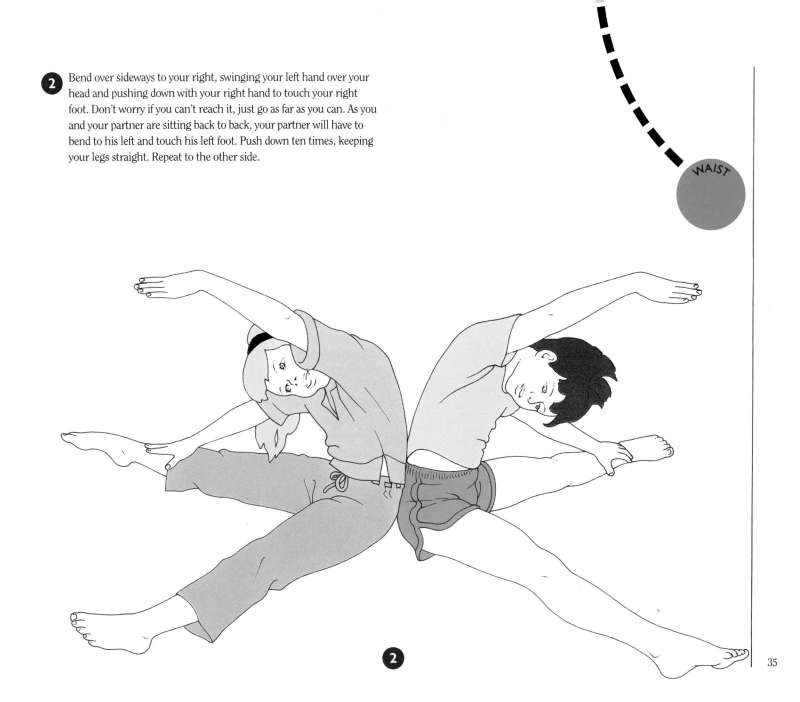

WAIST

2

YOGI BEAR

FOR ADULTS, AND CHILDREN FROM EIGHTEEN MONTHS.

Aim: to tone and firm waist and midriff.

1 Sit on the floor, back straight, with your legs wide apart. Bend your left leg and tuck your foot into the top of your thigh. This will give you good support as you bend sideways.

WAIST

1

2 Bend to your right, swinging your left arm over your head, and push your right hand down your leg as far as you can. Push down five times. Repeat the exercise to the left five times.

don't cheat by bending slightly backwards or forwards

2

CLOCKWORK YOGI BEAR

Get someone to wind you up and be a clockwork Yogi Bear.

Sit up straight, bend your knees, and take your feet round to the right. Raise your arms and clasp your hands together behind your head.

Keeping your hands together bend to the right up to ten times. Then get someone to re-wind you and repeat to the left.

TRIANGLE BUDDHA BEND

FOR ADULTS, AND CHILDREN FROM EIGHTEEN MONTHS.

Aim: stretches and works waist and back muscles.

I Sit on the floor with your back straight and your legs crossed like a buddha. Raise your arms and clasp your hands behind your head.

I

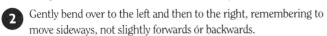

2 Gently bend over to the left and then to the right, remembering to move sideways, not slightly forwards or backwards.

TRIANGLE BUDDHA BEND 2

This variation stretches the leg muscles, too.

Sit on the floor with your legs straight, as wide apart as is comfortable, and clasp your hands behind your head. Bend sideways and touch your right leg with your right elbow, straighten up, then bend over and touch your left elbow to your left leg. Repeat up to ten times each side to begin with and gradually work up to twenty.

2

THE BALLERINA LUNGE

FOR ADULTS, AND CHILDREN FROM THREE YEARS.

Aim: gently stretches waist, upper arms and back. Good for releasing tension after hard waist exercises.

Don't just hurl yourself from left to right, but try to move with the grace and rhythm of a real dancer.

1 Stand with your feet apart, knees slightly bent and back straight but relaxed. Bend your left knee and lunge to the left, swinging your right arm round to the left and stretching to the left as far as you can. .

40 **1**

2 Turn and lunge to the right, stretching as far as you can. Repeat five times to each side.

WAIST

THE HAPPY PUP

FOR ADULTS, AND CHILDREN FROM EIGHTEEN MONTHS.

Aim: to strengthen and tone the muscles of the waist, lower back, thighs and buttocks.

If you watch a dog that is pleased and happy you'll see that he enthusiastically wags his tail from side to side. Wag your bottom like a real puppy – but not too quickly. Take care not to hollow or arch your back, but keep it quite straight.

1 Kneel on all fours, keeping your back as straight as possible, and slowly wag your bottom from side to side. To show just what a happy pup you are try to wag your tail as much as forty times.

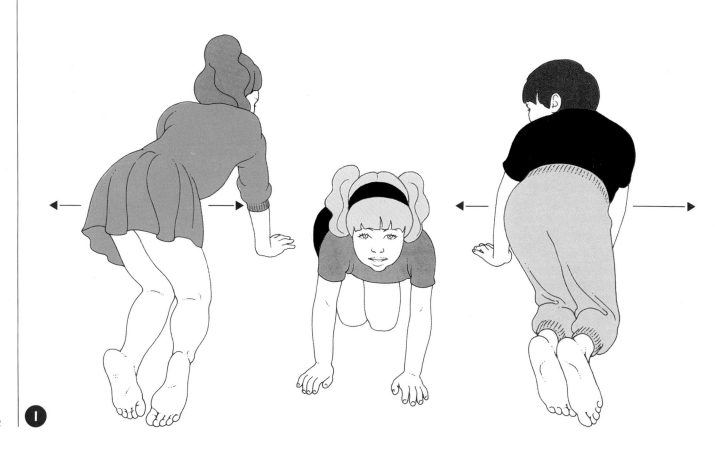

1

THE TWIST PRESS-UP

FOR ADULTS, AND CHILDREN FROM EIGHTEEN MONTHS.

Aim: tones and firms waistline, stretches the spine and arm and shoulder muscles.

This version of the press-up incorporates a twisting movement which works the waistline well.

1 Sit on the floor with your legs tucked round you. Your right leg should be folded back against your buttock, your left leg tucked against your right knee.

2 Keeping your back straight, twist your body round from the waist as far to the right as you can, resting your left hand on your right knee and your right hand on the floor as far round to the right as you can. Don't let your body slouch.

3 Slowly and smoothly swing back round to the left, and twist to the left, then lean over your right leg and, placing your hands on the floor directly under your shoulders, bend your elbows and push your body towards the floor as far as you can comfortably go. Repeat up to ten times, then change legs and do the same number of twist press-ups to the right.

1

2

twist to the right

twist back round to the left

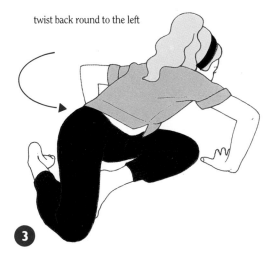

3

ROLLER BALL

INTRODUCTION

It is very important that we have strong tummy muscles. Weak tummy muscles are responsible for a large proportion of back pain – not weak back muscles. This especially applies to women who have had children. The lack of exercise in today's life-styles means that most of us have weak tummy muscles – which makes for bad posture, which causes back ache.

But the abdominal muscles are very difficult to exercise properly, and all too often we end up straining our backs instead of strengthening our tummies. For instance, when doing tummy exercises that involve lying on the floor (raising legs, sit-ups), you must always make sure that the small of your back is pressed firmly against the floor – *never* let it arch. This will ensure that your tummy does the work, not your back. If your tummy muscles are working effectively they will flatten as you exercise them, whereas if they are too weak they will tend to 'bulge' or 'peak'. If this happens stop the exercise as, again, it will be your lower back that is taking the strain. Stick to the easier exercises until you are stronger and fitter.

FOR ADULTS, AND CHILDREN FROM THREE YEARS.

Aim: tones tummy and thigh muscles, and helps to develop good co-ordination in children.

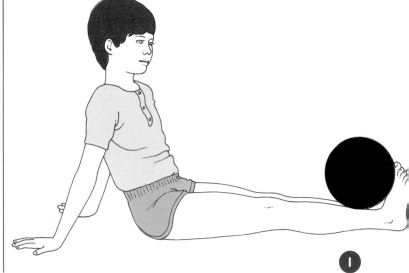

①

1. Sit on the floor with your legs stretched out in front of you, support yourself with your hands on the floor in a comfortable position. Place a ball on top of your feet.

2. Raise your legs so that the ball rolls down to the tops of your thighs.

3. Then lower your legs and raise yourself up on your arms, keeping them straight, so that the ball rolls down again to your feet.

45

BICYCLE MADE FOR TWO

FOR ADULTS, AND CHILDREN FROM EIGHTEEN MONTHS.

Aim: tones and strengthens tummy, thigh and calf muscles.

The closer in length your child's legs are to yours the easier this exercise will be. If you are pedalling with someone much smaller than you, don't place all your weight against their feet. Instead support most of the weight yourself – this will work your muscles extra hard.

Don't let your back arch as you pedal – keep it pressed flat against the floor to avoid placing strain on it.

1 Lie on the floor on your back. Raise your legs and place the soles of your feet against your partner's. Imagine you are riding a bicycle and, keeping your feet together at all times, pedal your legs in large circles. Change direction after ten pedals.

if your feet are very ticklish put your slippers on!

46

MOUNTAINEER

FOR ADULTS, AND CHILDREN FROM FOUR YEARS.

Aim: strengthens tummy muscles.

This is a sit-up exercise for the very strong and fit. If you find it hard to do, come back to it another time when you are more fit.

1 Lie on your back on the floor with your legs resting on your mother's thighs, your feet against her tummy.

2 Slowly and carefully sit up. Place your hands on your thighs, and inch your hands up your legs until you are sitting upright and your hands are touching your toes – or as near as they can get.

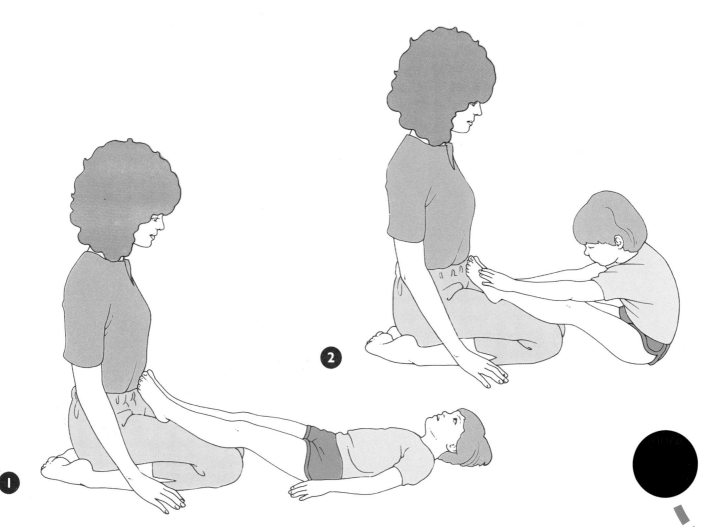

47

Boat race

FOR ADULTS, AND CHILDREN FROM FIVE YEARS.

Aim: Strengthens tummy and thigh muscles.

Have a boat race with your friends and family. Take it in turns to be coxswain and call 'in, out!' while the others heave the oars backwards and forwards.

1 Sit up with your back straight, knees bent and feet flat on the floor.

heave your imaginary oars back so you are balancing on your bottom

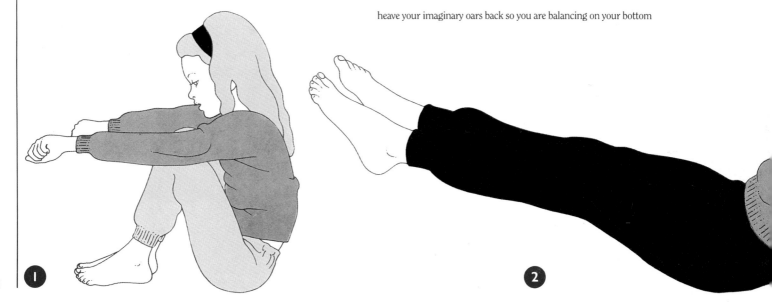

48 **1**

2

2 Now row the boat. Lifting your feet from the floor, balance on your bottom as you pull back your elbows and thrust your legs straight out in front of you.

3 Now push your oars out; thrust your arms out and pull your knees back against your chest, keeping your feet off the floor. Repeat up to ten times.

PENDULUM SWING

FOR ADULTS, AND CHILDREN FROM FOUR YEARS.

Aim: strengthens tummy and thigh muscles.

Pretend that your legs are the pendulum of an upside-down clock and swing them backwards and forwards. This is a difficult exercise and should only be attempted by the very fit.

1 Lie on your back with your arms at your sides, legs straight out.

2 Bend your knees up to your chest.

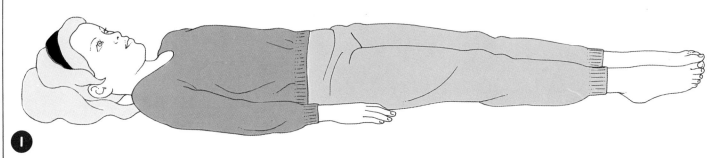

1

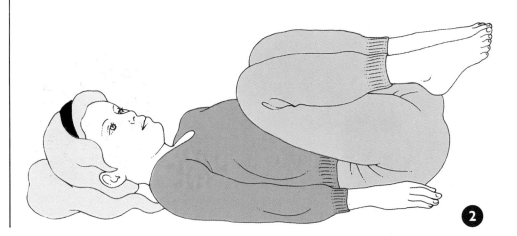

2

3 Straighten your knees and raise your legs up as high as you comfortably can, making a right angle. Then move your legs backwards and forwards (about 10° either side of the right angle) like a swinging pendulum.

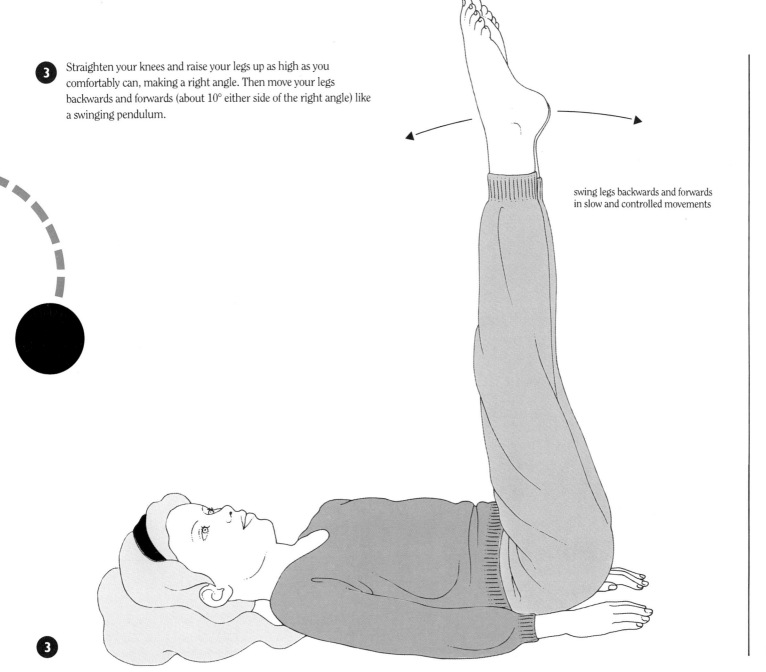

swing legs backwards and forwards in slow and controlled movements

3

51

MOONGLIDE

FOR ADULTS, AND CHILDREN FROM EIGHTEEN MONTHS.

Aim: strengthens tummy and inner thigh muscles.

Small children will find this exercise game easier to do with someone close to their own size. Remember to keep your back pressed against the floor.

1 Lie on your back on the floor opposite your partner. Place the soles of your feet together and straighten your legs so that they are raised into a pyramid shape.

2 Slowly and carefully open your legs as wide as you comfortably can, keeping the soles of your feet pressed together. Bring them back together again. Take care not to jerk your legs apart as this will hurt your muscles. Let your legs glide slowly; imagine they are gliding weightlessly into orbit to circle the moon. Repeat three times.

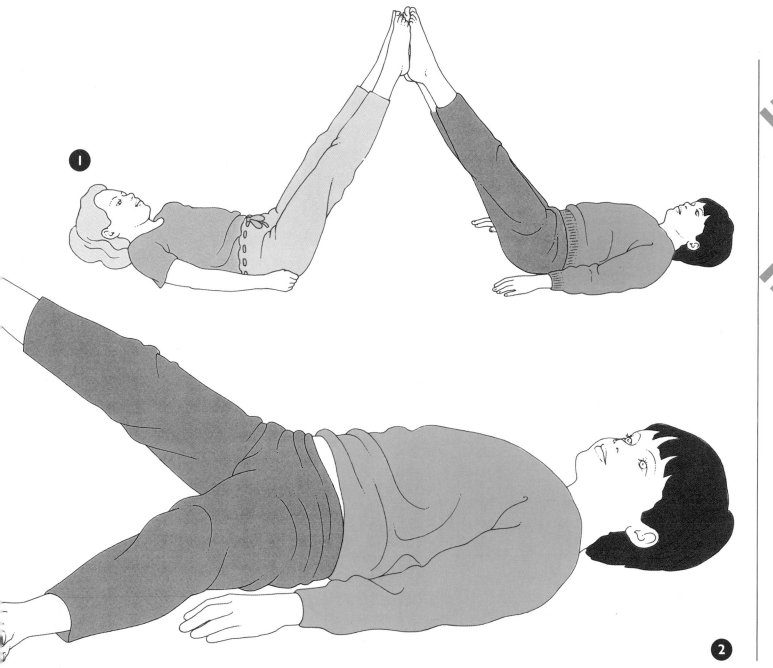

CATERPILLAR CURL

FOR ADULTS, AND CHILDREN FROM FIVE YEARS.

Aim: strengthens tummy muscles.

In this exercise you curl your body up like a caterpillar. It is very important that you keep your feet on the floor as you sit up – this ensures you are using your tummy muscles, not your back muscles.

1 Lie on your back, knees bent, feet flat on the floor, arms straight back either side of your head, and breathe in slowly.

2 Slowly and carefully sit up, breathing out gradually, swing your arms up over your head and hold them straight out in front of you at shoulder level. Slowly sink back to starting position.

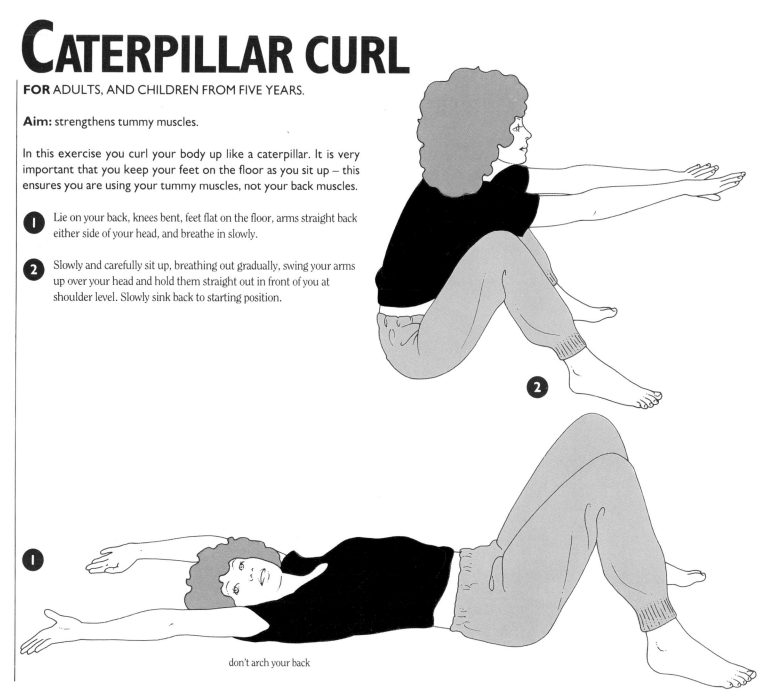

don't arch your back

3 With knees bent, feet flat on the floor, fold your arms across your chest and breathe in as before.

4 Slowly rise to sitting position and straighten your back. Breathe out as you sit up and take care not to let tummy muscles bulge.

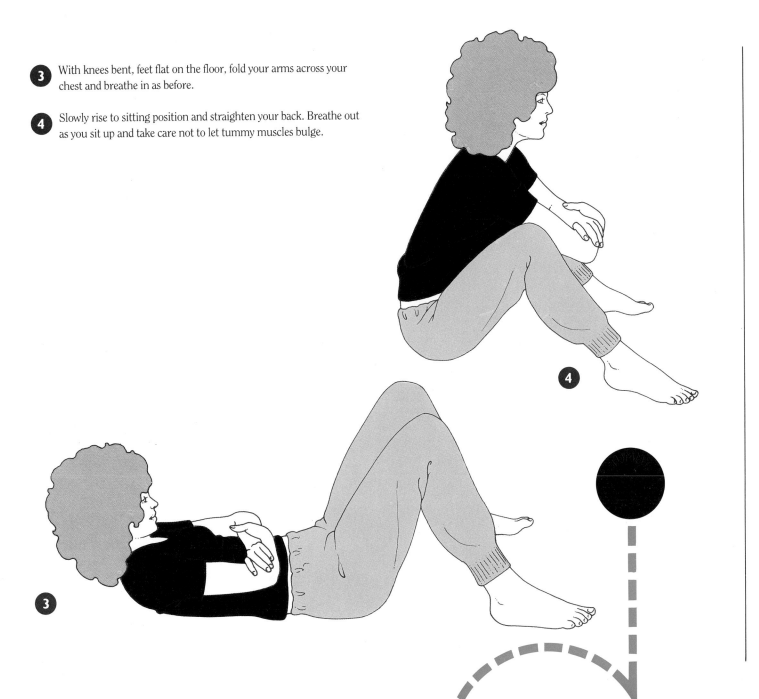

INTRODUCTION

Legs are made for walking, running, dancing, swimming, cycling, but mostly they only walk, and not that often thanks to cars and buses that take us where we want to go. So it is hardly surprising that our leg muscles waste away leaving us with flabby thighs and skinny calves. Women who have had children, in particular, find they lose much of the muscle tone of their thighs. The following exercise games use all the major muscles of the thighs and calves to keep your legs firm and supple, and your children's legs strong and sturdy.

STIFF SCISSORS

FOR ADULTS, AND CHILDREN FROM EIGHTEEN MONTHS.

Aim: firms and tightens thigh and calf muscles.

Partners should be of more or less equal size to make this game fair. If there is any discrepancy in strength, be careful.

1 Sit on the floor with your back straight, legs straight out in front of you and slightly apart. Support yourself by leaning back on your arms. Now get your partner to sit facing you, placing her legs either side of yours. Pretend your partners legs are a pair of scissors that have got stuck and try to prise the scissors open by pushing her legs apart with yours. Change places and repeat.

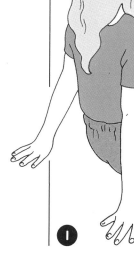

1

JUMPING FROG RACE

FOR ADULTS, AND CHILDREN FROM THREE YEARS.

Aim: strengthens leg muscles, gives the whole body a good stretch and stirs up the circulation. Helps children to develop good co-ordination and balance.

❶ From a crouching position, spring up into the air and stretch your arms high above your head, before returning to the starting position.

See who can leap the farthest and fastest.

Humpty Dumpty

FOR ADULTS, AND CHILDREN FROM EIGHTEEN MONTHS.

Aim: strengthens and tones thigh and calf muscles.

Children love this game, and it encourages the more timid child to be less afraid of physical activity and enjoy a rough and tumble. Adults should take care not to arch their backs, but keep them flat.

1 Lie on your back on a bed or lots of soft cushions. Bend your knees up against your chest and take hold of your child's hands.

2 Support your child with your hands as he sits astride your legs and bounce him up and down to the words of 'Humpty Dumpty'.

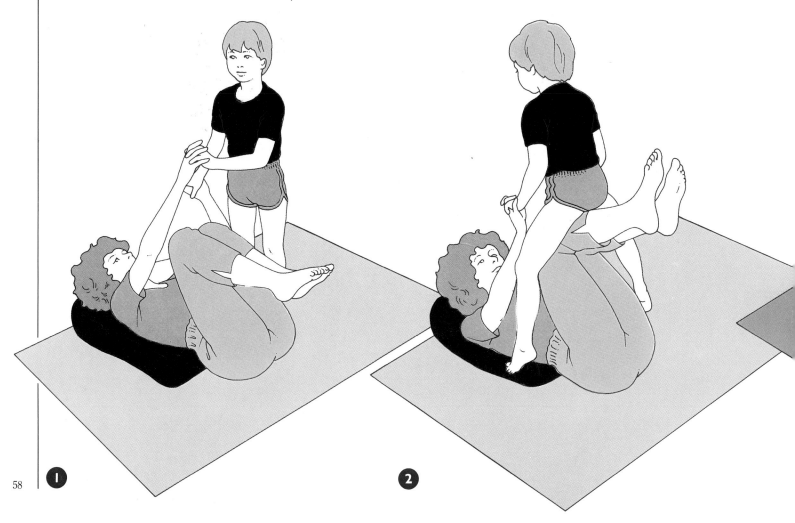

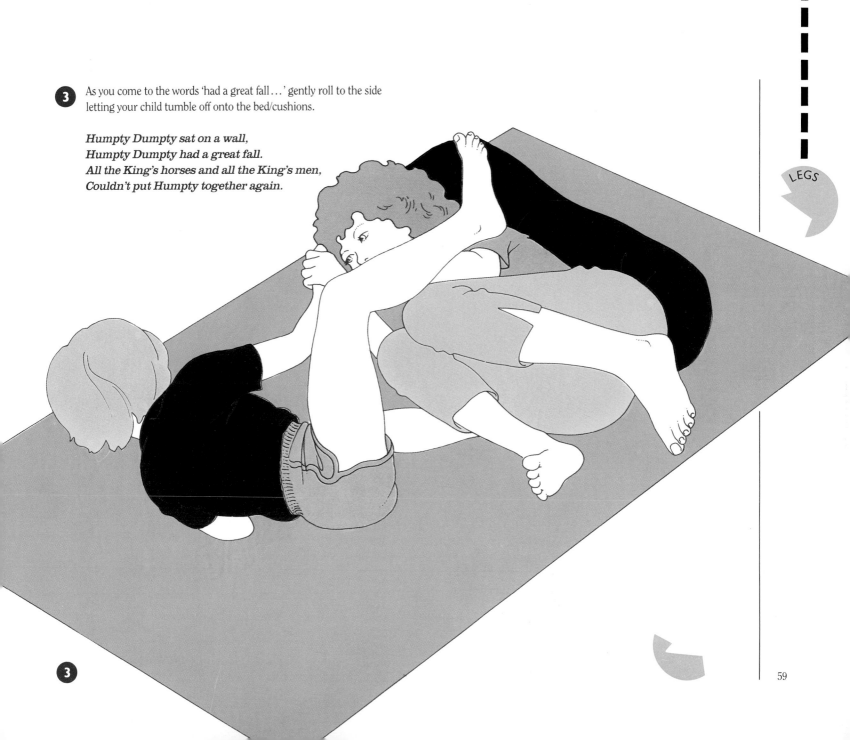

3 As you come to the words 'had a great fall...' gently roll to the side letting your child tumble off onto the bed/cushions.

Humpty Dumpty sat on a wall,
Humpty Dumpty had a great fall.
All the King's horses and all the King's men,
Couldn't put Humpty together again.

LEGS

Horsey, Horsey

FOR ADULTS, AND CHILDREN FROM TWO YEARS.

Aim: For adults – strengthens thigh and calf muscles. For children – encourages balancing prowess.

This game isn't just fun for children, it is an excellent exercise for adult thighs.

1 Lift your child onto your lap facing outwards and hold him/her firmly round the waist.

2 Slowly lift your knees up and down in turn as you chant the rhyme. Gradually increase the pace and your movements as you break into a trot, then into a canter.

3 Finally, the horse breaks into a gallop – bounce your child vigorously up and down on your knees.

4 Finish with 'and then he/she fell off' and gently lower your child to the floor.

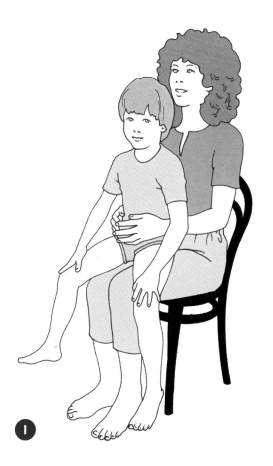

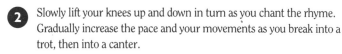

LEGS

That is the way the ladies ride,
Tri, tre, tre, tree, tri, tre, tre, tree,
This is the way the ladies ride,
Tri, tre tre tre, tre, tri-tre-tre-tree!

This is the way the gentlemen ride,
Gallop-a-trot, gallop-a-trot,
This is the way the gentlemen ride,
Gallop-a-gallop-a-trot!

This is the way the farmers ride,
Hobbledy-hoy, hobbledy-hoy,
This is the way the farmers ride,
Hobbledy, hobbledy-hoy!

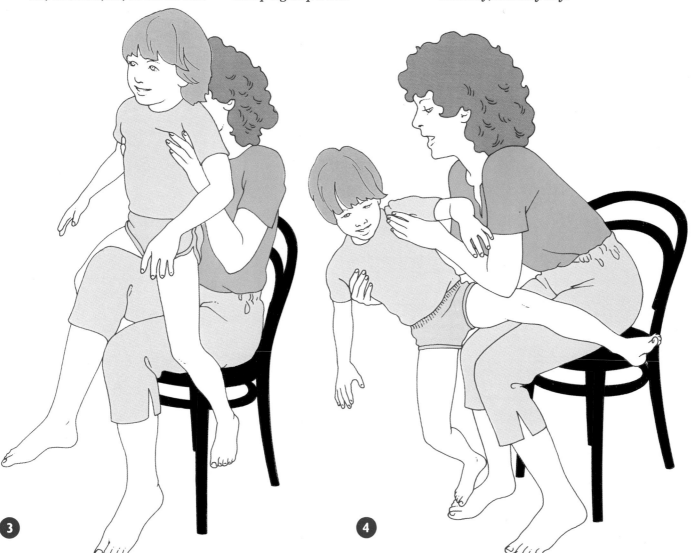

Hold a Ball

FOR ADULTS, AND CHILDREN FROM EIGHTEEN MONTHS.

Aim: strengthens inner thigh muscles and stretches hamstrings.

Try to keep the ball between your heels as you bend to touch your toes. Keep the small of your back as rounded as possible when you bend from the waist.

1 Stand up straight and grip a large round ball between your heels, pointing your feet slightly outwards.

2 Bend down and try to touch your toes without releasing the ball. *Don't* force yourself, only bend as far as you comfortably can.

LEGS

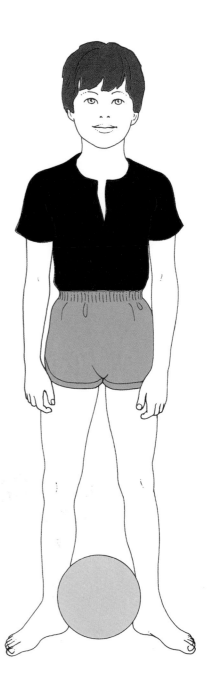

1

2

TUG A BALL

This exercise also works your inner thigh muscles. This time grip the ball between your knees and get a friend to try and pull it free. Grip the ball as tightly as you can. Then change places.

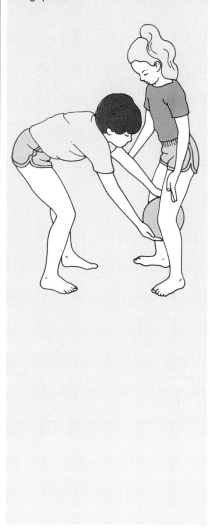

RING-A-RING-A-TULIPS

FOR ADULTS, AND CHILDREN FROM TWO YEARS.

Aim: strengthens thigh muscles.

A less abandoned version of Ring-a-Ring-a-Roses which requires greater muscle control.

1 Hold hands and skip round in a circle chanting 'Ring-a-Ring-a-Tulips'.

2 When you come to 'we all fall down' instead of hurling yourself to the floor, slowly sink down into a low squatting position without poking your bottom out and keeping your back very straight.

3 Slowly, without wobbling and with your back straight, rise up again – like a tulip!

Ring-a-ring-a-roses,
A pocket full of posies,
Atishoo! Atishoo!
We all fall down.

slowly sink down into a squatting position

rise up slowly without wobbling

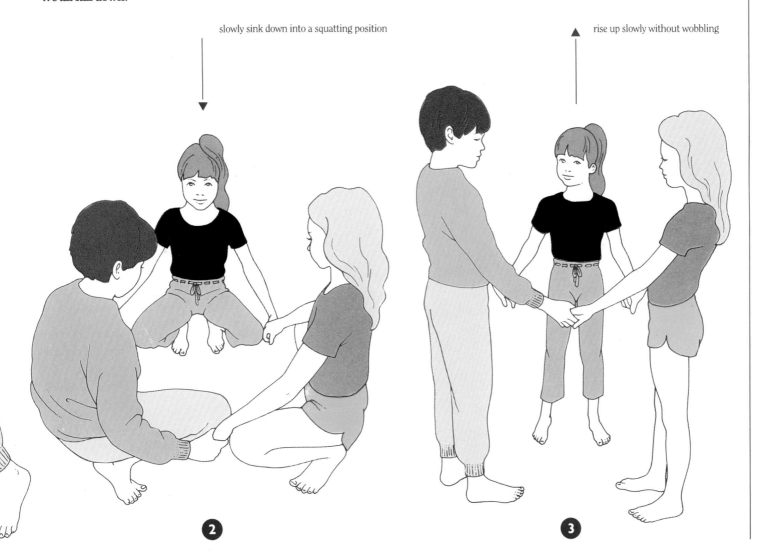

2

3

65

SUPERKID

FOR CHILDREN FROM THREE YEARS.

Aim: For adults – tones and strengthens thigh, calf and tummy muscles. For children – helps develop good balance.

Children love this exercise – they find it really exciting to balance on your feet in mid-air like a real gymnast! As they gain confidence they may like to let go of your hands and balance on their own. But don't encourage timid children to do this before they feel ready, let them go at their own pace. Only the most supple adults will be able to straighten their legs completely as in step 3, don't force yourself if you find it hard. When balancing older or heavier children *always* keep your knees bent. Be ready to support your child if necessary.

① Lie on your back and bend your knees and raise your feet so that your child can rest her tummy, or wherever is the most comfortable, against them.

② Then, holding her hands to steady and support her, slowly and carefully straighten your legs, raising her upwards.

③ As you both get more confident your child might feel like letting go of your hands and 'flying' like Superman!

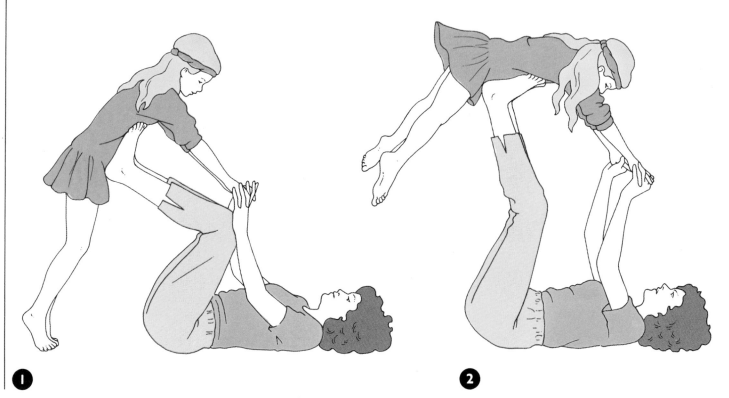

①

②

'Supermen' should hold their bodies as straight as possible in true 'flying' position!

legs and arms should be spread out wide to help balance

adults arms should be spread out flat on the floor to help balance; the small of the back should be against the floor, not arched

3

ONE-LEGGED SUPERKID

As you gain strength you could try to raise your child with one leg. Follow the instructions as for two legs, but take care to position your foot so it is comfortable. Keep your other leg bent, your foot flat on the floor.

SUPERTOT

When balancing a small child keep your knees bent slightly lower so that you can hold his hands to prevent him falling.

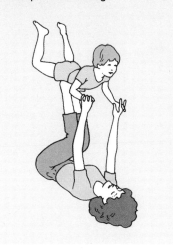

THE INSECT

FOR ADULTS, AND CHILDREN FROM TWO YEARS.

Aim: strengthens and stretches hamstrings and thighs.

Pretend to be an insect, it will help to develop your balancing skills.

1 With your feet quite wide apart, bend your knees and place your hands on the floor in front of you.

1

2

2 Then raise your heels as you move your bottom in a large circle, down, up and forwards, twice. If you can't keep your hands flat on the floor, just let them touch the floor.

straighten your legs a little as you raise your bottom

don't worry if you can't keep your hands flat, just touch the floor with your fingers

2

Now do the Wasp Bounce – you've probably seen wasps do this as they gorge on gooey cakes.

Squat down with your legs quite wide apart. Put your arms between your knees and place your hands on the floor behind your feet. Press your elbows against the inside of your legs to stretch your thighs open as far as possible. Now do the wasp bounce and gently bounce your bottom up and down.

Bouncy Legs

FOR ADULTS, AND CHILDREN FROM EIGHTEEN MONTHS.

Aim: to release tension in legs after exercising.

1 Any time your legs feel stiff just lie back on the floor with your hands by your sides. (Remember to keep the small of your back pressed against the floor.) Raise your knees up to your chest and try to kick your bottom. Lie in a row with your friends and be a chorus line.

LEGS

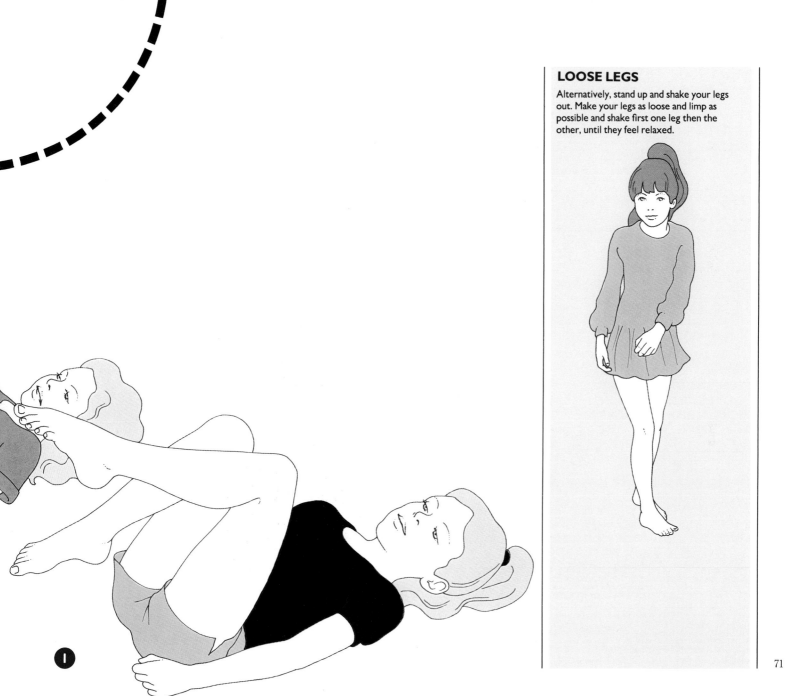

LOOSE LEGS

Alternatively, stand up and shake your legs out. Make your legs as loose and limp as possible and shake first one leg then the other, until they feel relaxed.

1

INTRODUCTION

Due to lack of exercise buttocks don't always stay where they should. All too often they spread, creeping round to make bulges on the hips, and downwards so that they run into the thighs, losing shape and firmness; if yours don't, the following exercise games will work hips, buttocks and backs of thighs in order to firm up the whole area.

BALL GAME

FOR ADULTS, AND CHILDREN FROM EIGHTEEN MONTHS.

Aim: works buttock, inner leg and tummy muscles.

Play a ball game with your feet. Use a big, soft round ball that is easy to catch with your feet.

1 Sit on the floor opposite your partner. Hold a ball between your feet, and place your hands on the floor to support yourself. Then bend your knees and throw the ball to your partner, who must catch it with their feet, then throw it back to you.

2 If there are three of you, one can be referee and take the place of the first person to drop the ball.

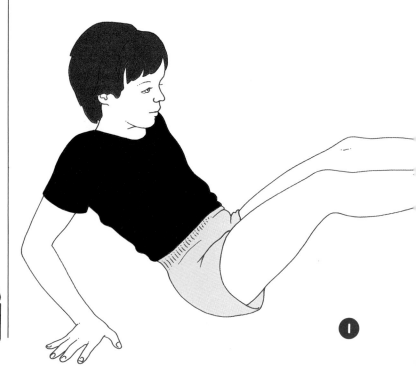

ROCK AND ROLL

FOR ADULTS, AND CHILDREN FROM FOUR YEARS.

Aim: tones buttocks and thighs.

Rock and roll your way round a carpet, and in summer try rocking and rolling on your bottom across the grass.

1 Sit on the floor, keeping your back as straight as you can. Bend your knees and place the soles of your feet together. Now hold your feet.

1

2 Rock from one buttock to the other, rolling sideways as far as possible without actually falling over.

BOTTOMS

2

75

BUM RACE

FOR ADULTS, AND CHILDREN FROM FOUR YEARS.

Aim: strengthens buttock, tummy and leg muscles.

This race appeals to every child's sense of fun. They find it hilarious to charge across the floor on their bottoms. And of course these movements are excellent for mothers to help tone up the dimply flesh that tends to accumulate on thighs and buttocks – often known as 'cellulite'. Run forwards (this chiefly exercises the tummy muscles), then run backwards (to exercise the buttock muscles). Decide on a finishing point for your race, such as a piece of furniture, or where the carpet ends.

who can win the Bum Race?

BOTTOMS

1

1 Sit on the floor with your legs straight out in front of you. When everyone is in position shout, 'Ready, steady, go!'

2 Move across the floor by shifting your weight from one buttock to the other, inching your way forwards as fast as you can. Then do the race in reverse and wobble backwards to the starting point.

SAILING

FOR ADULTS, AND CHILDREN FROM THREE YEARS.

Aim: for adults – works and strengthens buttocks and thighs. For children – helps develop good balance and works tummy and leg muscles.

This exercise is quite hard to do, but it gets easier with practice. When pushing your hips up take care not to arch your back but keep your body as straight as possible and buttocks tightly clenched.

1 Lie on your back, knees bent, feet flat on the floor. Your child should sit astride your pelvis where it feels most comfortable, with his feet on the floor. Hold his hands throughout the exercise game to help balance and support him.

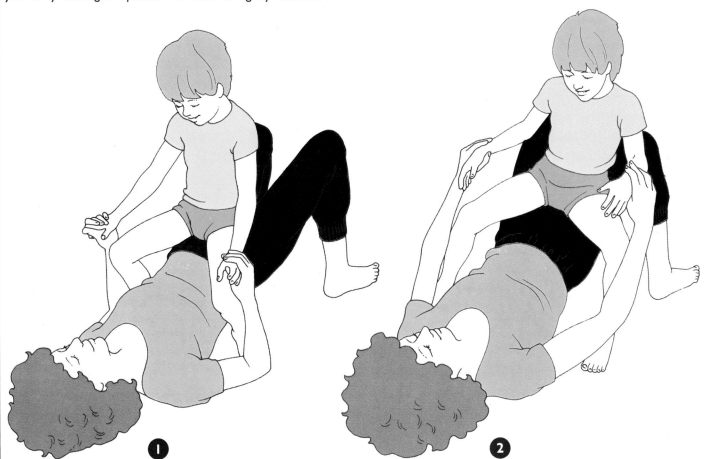

2 Push your pelvis up, off the floor, transferring your weight to your shoulders and feet. Resist the temptation to arch your back as you push up; keep it as straight as you can.

3 Make undulating, wave-like movements with your hips as you move them down and up to the side and then down and up to the other side, giving your child a ride in a boat on a rough sea.

try not to arch your back – keep your body as straight as possible

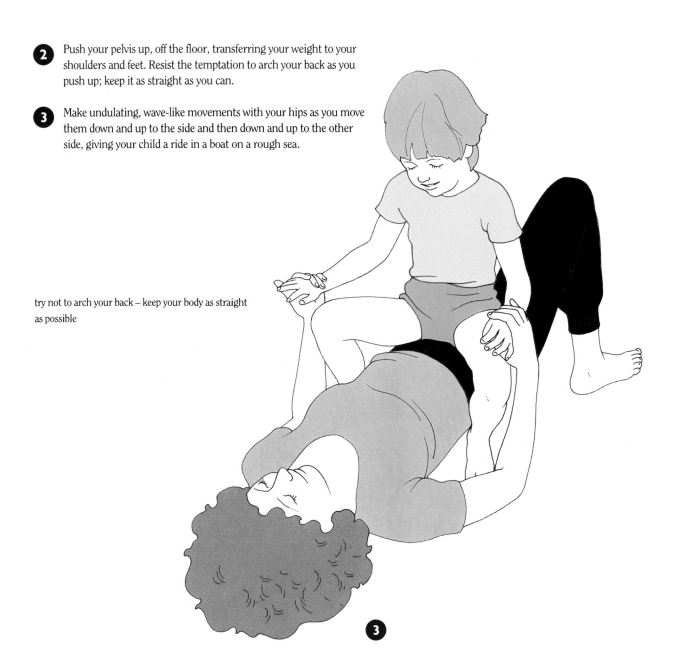

3

79

THE BOTTOM BALANCE

FOR ADULTS, AND CHILDREN FROM THREE YEARS.

Aim: strengthens and tones buttocks, upper thighs and tummy muscles.

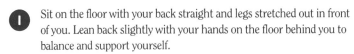

1 Sit on the floor with your back straight and legs stretched out in front of you. Lean back slightly with your hands on the floor behind you to balance and support yourself.

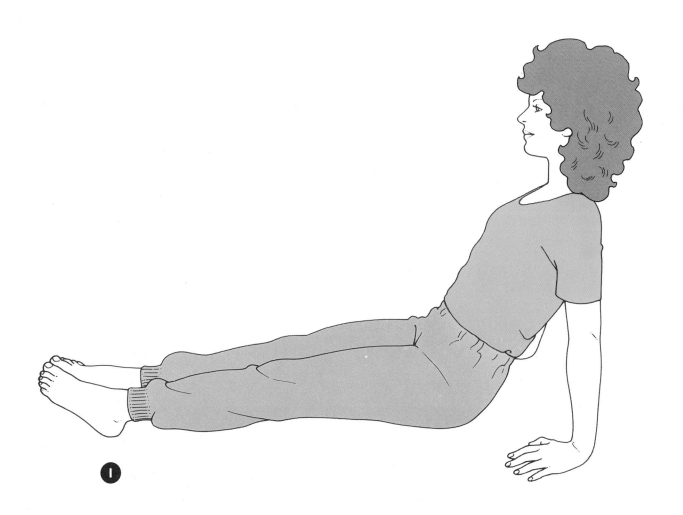

2 Press down on your hands as you tilt your body back and lift your legs up off the floor together and hold them there for a moment, keeping them as straight as you can. Breathe normally.

BOTTOMS

hold your body in a wide 'V' shape

2

ADVANCED BOTTOM BALANCE

To make balancing on your bottom even more difficult, don't use your arms for support. Instead, hold a soft toy in your arms.

Sit on the floor with your legs in front of you. Lean back and raise your legs off the ground. Keep your back rounded and legs as straight as you can and balance only on your bottom.

SQUEEZE THE BOT

FOR ADULTS, AND CHILDREN FROM FIVE YEARS.

Aim: tones buttock and thigh muscles.

If your child is under five maybe he would like to crawl through the arch you make with your body.

1 Lie on your back, arms by your sides with your legs comfortably apart, knees bent and feet flat on the floor. Relax.

2 Breathe in and slowly and carefully shift your weight onto your shoulders and feet as you lift your bottom up. Don't arch your back, but keep your body in as straight a line as possible from shoulders to knees. Then push up, clenching and squeezing the cheeks of your buttocks tightly.

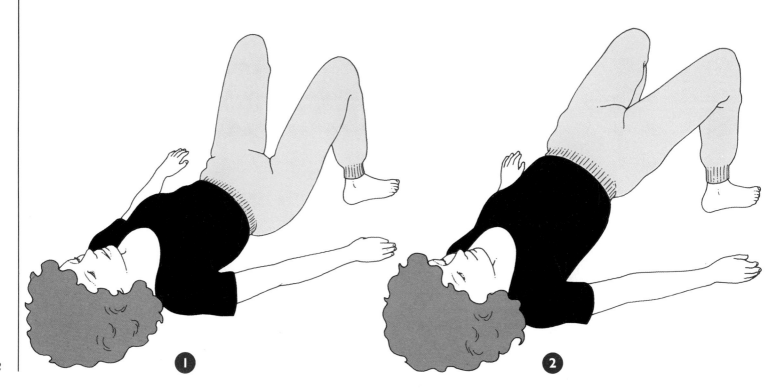

THE MUSTANG

FOR ADULTS, AND CHILDREN FROM FOUR YEARS.

Aim: strengthens and tones buttocks and thighs.

Mustangs are wild horses in America that cannot be ridden until they have been broken in. Pretend you are a mustang with a rider on your back and try to kick him off.

❶ Get down on your hands and knees and lift your knee out sideways, then try to kick your bottom with your foot – that should get the rider off! Change legs and repeat.

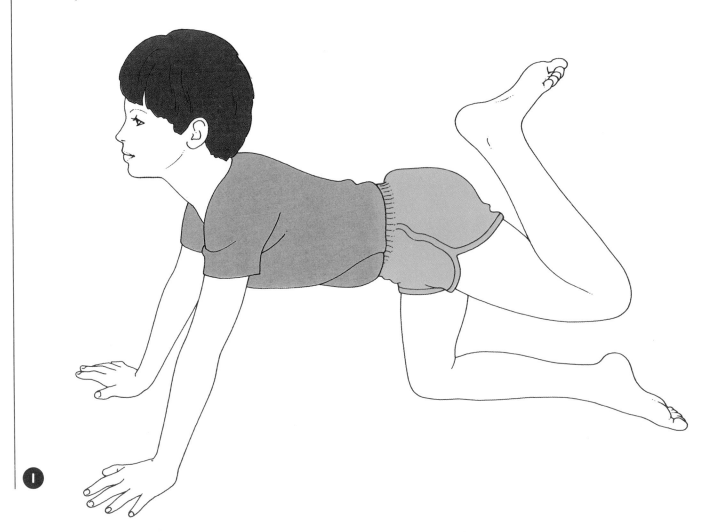

❶

83

INTRODUCTION

An aerobic section is included because it is so popular with adults, and children love all the jumping about.

Never do aerobics if you are pregnant, severely over-weight, over forty, or haven't done any exercise for years. Also, never if you have any heart problems or high blood pressure, have just recovered from flu, a cold or any viral illness.

Aerobic means 'with air'; any exercise that increases your pulse rate and forces more oxygen into the lungs is aerobic. To benefit the heart and lungs, aerobic exercises should be sustained for only ten minutes at a time. The exercise games should only make you slightly out of breath; if you find you can hardly breathe, you are overdoing it and should stick to the easier exercise games until you are fitter.

As with all exercises, aerobics should never hurt; always stop if you feel any pain, however slight. This especially applies to children, who may overdo it if not supervised.

Your metabolic rate (the rate at which you burn calories) will rise while doing aerobics, and stay high for hours afterwards, so aerobic exercise is an excellent way to shed excess weight, and keep it off.

Doctors have been alarmed by the number of injuries that result from over-strenuous aerobics classes. This is why I have begun this aerobic section with gentle stretching exercises to get you going gradually.

AEROBIC REACH

FOR ADULTS, AND CHILDREN FROM EIGHTEEN MONTHS.

Aim: stretches muscles of arms, shoulders, back and thighs.

 Stand with your feet apart, knees slightly bent, back straight, tummy in and bottom tucked under. Stretch your arms up above your head and reach up as high as you can, first with one hand, then the other. Sway from one side to the other each time you stretch upwards, to give your legs a stretch, too.

BALLERINA SWING

FOR ADULTS, AND CHILDREN FROM EIGHTEEN MONTHS.

Aim: stretches arms, shoulders, back and legs.

Really stretch your arms up and get into a good rhythm as you swing your body from side to side. Remember to breathe deeply and evenly; breathe in as you swing your arms up, and out as you bring them down and turn to the other side.

1 Stand with your back straight, tummy in and bottom tucked under, legs apart and knees bent. Then swing your arms up above your head as you lunge to the left.

2 Take your arms down as you straighten up and swing your arms up above your head, as before, when you lunge to the right.

turn and swing your arms up to the right

DISCO DANCER

FOR ADULTS, AND CHILDREN FROM EIGHTEEN MONTHS.

Aim: increases your heartbeat to stir up circulation and speed up metabolism.

1 Play a track of your favourite disco music and dance to it until the track ends (three minutes).

TWIST AGAIN

FOR ADULTS, AND CHILDREN FROM FOUR YEARS.

Aim: works the waistline and leg muscles and speeds up heartbeat and circulation.

1 Stand up straight with tummy in and bottom tucked under, feet slightly apart and knees lightly bent. Now jump up and down twisting your hips to the right on the first jump, and then to the left on the next jump. Repeat ten times.

1

1

JOGGER

FOR ADULTS, AND CHILDREN FROM EIGHTEEN MONTHS.

Aim: exercises the legs and stirs up a sluggish circulation.

Jogging is one of the most popular aerobic exercises — you often see joggers pounding round the block trying to get fit.

1   Be a jogger and jog on the spot forty times.

1

89

Starfish

Aim: stretches the whole body and works the legs.

While this exercise takes a lot of energy, don't do it too aggressively or you might strain your muscles.

1 Stand up straight with your feet comfortably apart and jump into the air, shooting out your arms and legs as wide as you can to make a starfish shape. Repeat five times.

90

JUMP TOGETHER

FOR ADULTS, AND CHILDREN FROM FOUR YEARS.

Aim: gets the circulation going and works the legs.

1 Hold hands with your partner and jump up and down together as high as you can. Really put a lot of spring into your jumps and always land gently on toes, then heels, with knees bent. Jump together five to ten times.

91

CAT'S GOT THE MEASLES

FOR ADULTS, AND CHILDREN FROM FOUR YEARS.

Aim: exercises feet and leg muscles and speeds up heartbeat and circulation.

If there are more than two of you playing Cat's got the Measles, stand in a circle together.

1 Stand opposite your partner with your feet apart.

2 Jump up as high as you can, crossing your legs in mid-air so you land with your feet crossed.

3 Jump up again and uncross your feet and land with your feet apart.

Now chant this rhyme as you jump up and down in time, crossing and uncrossing your legs.

Cat's got the measles,
Dog's got the flu,
Chicken's got the chicken pox,
And so have you!

Those who land with their feet crossed at the end of the rhyme are out. When there are only two of you playing, see who can win most out of three games.

1

land with your feet crossed

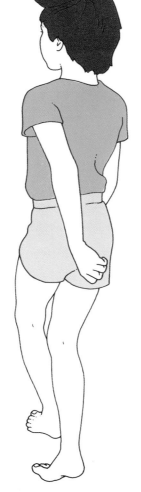

now land with your feet apart

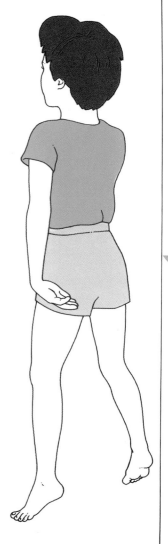

INTRODUCTION

Hands and feet need exercising, too. The following exercise games will help improve dexterity and balancing skills — good for those who tend to be clumsy. The exercises will strengthen the small muscles of the hands and feet, and improve circulation, which will help to discourage chilblains in cold weather.

SNAPDRAGONS

FOR ADULTS, AND CHILDREN FROM EIGHTEEN MONTHS.

Aim: to make hands more supple and strong.

1 Stand in a comfortable position, bend your elbows and make your hands into tight fists.

2 Snap your hands open as strongly as you can and make great big snapdragons. Repeat five times, then shake your hands out to release tension and repeat another five times.

HAND TINGLER

FOR ADULTS, AND CHILDREN FROM EIGHTEEN MONTHS.

Aim: works shoulders and arms and improves circulation in hands.

Make your hands tingle as you swing your arms round in big wide circles. Your movements should be slow and controlled – if you go too fast you will pull or strain muscles.

1. Stand up straight, bottom tucked under and feet comfortably apart.

2. Swing your right arm up, back and round in a big circle. Repeat three times.

3. Change arms and swing your left arm round three times.

1

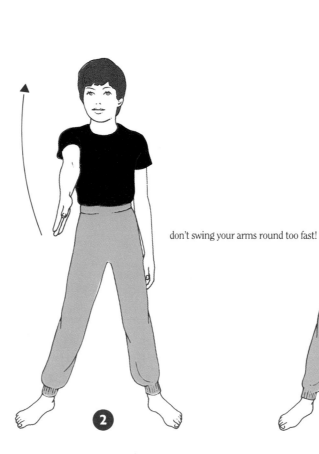

don't swing your arms round too fast!

2

3

INDIAN COPYCAT DANCE

FOR ADULTS, AND CHILDREN FROM EIGHTEEN MONTHS.

Aim: exercises hands and finger joints, and works leg muscles.

To look like the Hindu goddess Kali with many arms, do the Copycat Dance with your whole family or some friends. Stand with your legs wide apart and knees bent. The shortest of you should stand in front, increasing in size towards the back. Wear masks on your faces to make the dance look more authentic and move your hands as gracefully as you can, flexing and twisting them in and out. The person in front improvises the movements and the ones behind try to copy as closely as possible.

1 Pretend you are an Indian dancer and imitate the delicate hand movements they make. Place the first finger and thumb of each hand together and gently twist and flex your hands. Change fingers and take each finger in turn to your thumb as you twist your hands, making fluid movements outwards and back towards your face.

HANDS AND FEET

1

96

EVERY WITCH WAY

FOR ADULTS, AND CHILDREN FROM FOUR YEARS.

Aim: encourages children to straighten their bodies, helps develop good balance and exercises the small muscles of the feet.

1 The child should stand as straight as possible, pretending to be an inflexible board. An adult should sit in front and behind her and gently push the child backwards and forwards between them. The child must allow herself to be pushed backwards and forwards between the two witches without bending. If the child bends in any way the witches will put a spell on her.

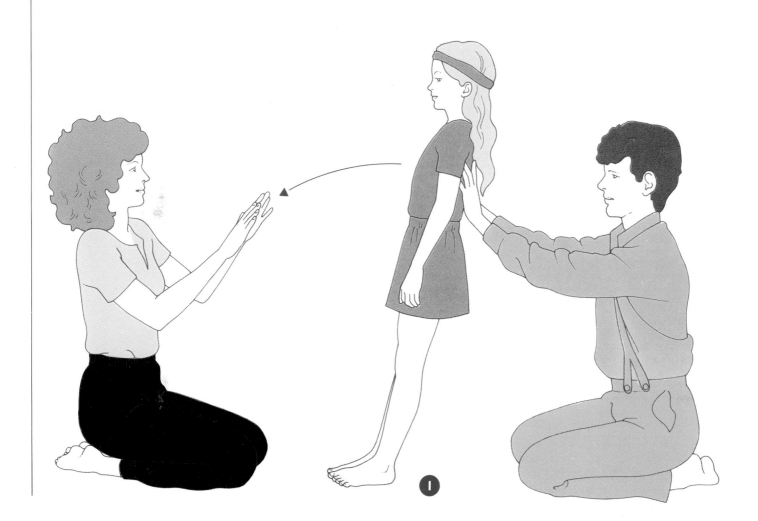

1

97

PERCY TOER

FOR ADULTS, AND CHILDREN FROM EIGHTEEN MONTHS.

Aim: exercises feet and toes, making them more supple and strong.

1 Help your parents to do the gardening by plucking out the weeds with your toes. Put them all neatly into a bucket as you work.

how many weeds can you pull up?

1

TIDY TOES

FOR ADULTS, AND CHILDREN FROM THREE YEARS.

Aim: strengthens small muscles of the feet.
Small children will want to put these tiny objects into their mouths
and up their noses – so don't let them play this game unsupervised.

❶ Empty a collection of small (but not sharp) stones, marbles or
buttons onto the floor; provide a box for each person playing. Now
tidy up by picking up as many things as you can with your toes and
putting them into your box. The person who has the most pieces in
their box when the floor is cleared is the winner.

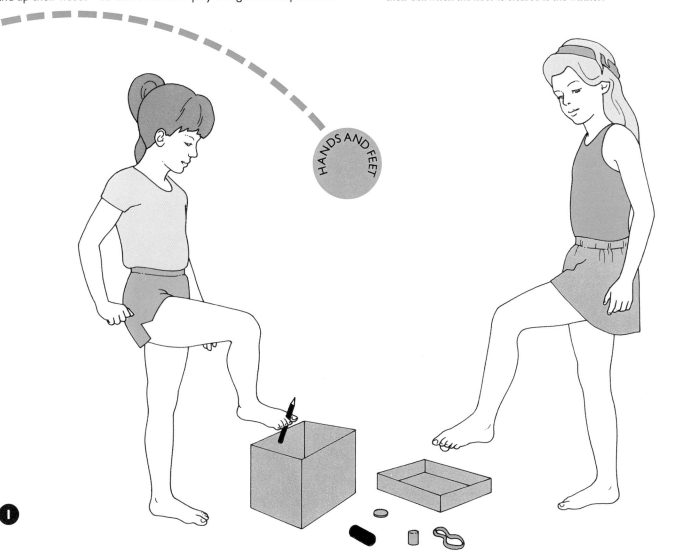

HANDS AND FEET

PASS THE PENCIL

FOR ADULTS, AND CHILDREN FROM EIGHTEEN MONTHS.

Aim: strengthens and exercises the small muscles of the feet.

1 Sit on the floor with your back straight and put your hands on the floor behind you to support yourself.

2 Pick up a pencil between your toes and pass it to a friend, who takes it with their toes. If there are lots of you playing, pass it round in a circle; the one who drops it is out.

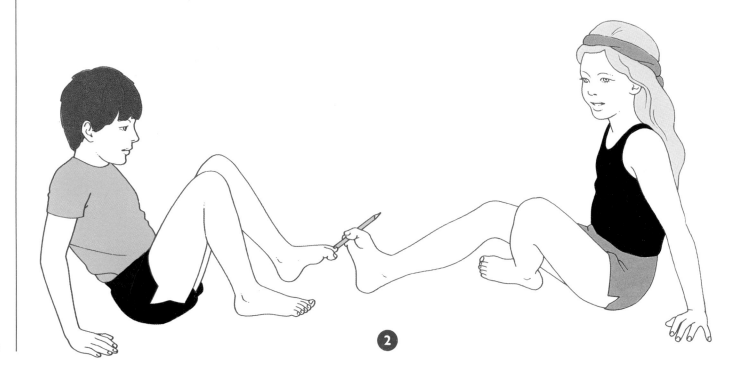

2

TIGHTROPE

FOR ADULTS, AND CHILDREN FROM EIGHTEEN MONTHS.

Aim: exercises the small muscles of the feet and helps children to develop good balance.

As your child walks the tightrope, help her to imagine she is a hundred feet above the crowds by supplying gasps of admiration.

1 Stretch a skipping rope, or any thick, soft piece of rope, along the floor and, with bare feet, walk the tightrope.

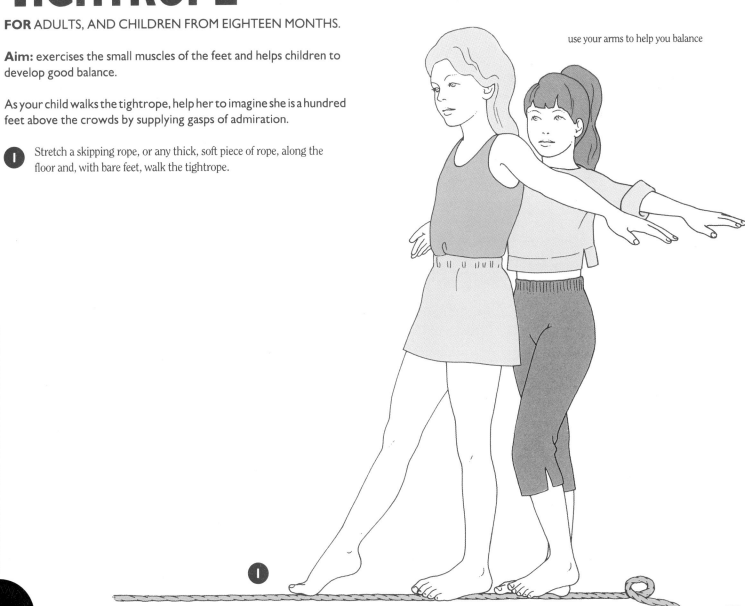

use your arms to help you balance

101

FOOTSIE WOOTSIE WORKOUT

FOR ADULTS, AND CHILDREN FROM EIGHTEEN MONTHS.

Aim: strengthens muscles of the feet and legs.

A complete workout routine for the feet.

1 Sit on the floor with your legs straight out in front of you. Lean back on your hands to support yourself. Spread your toes apart as if they were fingers – see who can open and stretch their toes the widest.

2 Sit on the floor as before but stretch and point your feet downwards towards the floor like a ballerina's toes as far as you can go. Do this eight times.

1

2

3 This time draw circles with your feet. Cross your ankles, point your toes and draw as big a circle as you can with first one foot then with the other. Then circle both feet inwards together four times, then circle them outwards four times.

3

HOKEY COKEY

Do the Hokey Cokey and shake your hands and feet out in turn.

YOGA LIONS

INTRODUCTION

Many of the earlier exercise games require a good sense of balance, which not everyone possesses. The following yoga-based exercises will help to make you more supple, give you more control over your body and thus make it better balanced.

FOR ADULTS, AND CHILDREN FROM EIGHTEEN MONTHS.

Aim: exercises the tongue, mouth and jaw.

1 Sit in a row on the floor with your legs crossed and your hands resting on your knees. Open your mouth as wide as possible and push your tongue out as far as you can – try to touch your chin. Make your hands into claws and stretch them out and roar like a lion. Roar three times and see who can be the fiercest lion in the jungle.

AMAZONIAN BOAT PROW

FOR ADULTS, AND CHILDREN FROM FIVE YEARS.

Aim: strengthens arms, shoulders and pectorals and stretches the spine.

Only the supple and strong should attempt this exercise – don't try it if you have any back problems. Don't force yourself into this press-up, but rise up just as far as you comfortably can.

1 Lie on your front with your legs straight and together and place your hands on the floor directly under your shoulders.

2 Breathe in and slowly and carefully straighten your arms, pushing your trunk up from the floor.

3 If you are very supple and fit, raise your body till your arms are straight; your legs should touch the floor throughout the exercise. See who can be the proudest boat prow. Breathe out as you slowly and carefully lower yourself down again.

YOGA

3

THE BOW

FOR ADULTS, AND CHILDREN FROM FIVE YEARS.

Aim: tones the arms, legs, pectorals, waist and back and makes the spine more supple.

Don't attempt this exercise if you have any problems with your back. This exercise is only for the very fit and supple as you bend your body backwards into the shape of a bow.

1 Lie on your front, legs slightly apart. Bend your knees, bringing your feet back towards your bottom. With your hands, reach back and take hold of your ankles or feet.

2 Breathe in as you raise your head and shoulders from the floor and lift your legs and feet upwards, still grasping them with your hands.

3 Feel your body stretch as you curve your body back, bringing your head and feet as close together as possible. Breathe in as you release your feet, and slowly relax back onto the floor.

bend your body back into the shape of a bow

3

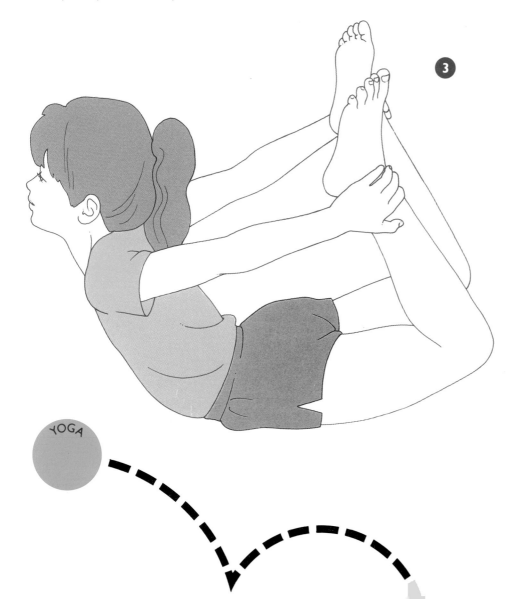

YOGA

THE BOW ROCK

When you can be a perfect Bow, try holding the Bow position and pushing your weight backwards and forwards to rock your body like a rocking horse. Push backwards and forwards once, then relax with your arms by your sides, legs straight out behind you, with your head on its side.

ICE SKATER'S ARABESQUE

FOR ADULTS, AND CHILDREN FROM FIVE YEARS.

Aim: helps develop good balance and gives the whole body a good stretch. Also works the small muscles of the weight-bearing foot.

Don't worry if you can't raise your legs very high at first or if you wobble and lose balance. You'll improve with practice.

1 Stand up straight with your feet together. Bend your left knee behind you and take hold of your left foot with your left hand. Raise your right arm to help balance yourself.

2 Find your balance, then slowly begin to extend your left leg, still holding your left foot with your hand. Stretch your right arm up and out in front of you.

3 Draw your body out into a beautiful curve as you stretch your right arm up and pull your left leg right back and up with your left arm. Keep your supporting leg as straight and still as possible. Now change legs and repeat.

110

THE TREE

FOR ADULTS, AND CHILDREN FROM FIVE YEARS.

Aim: helps to develop good balance and works the small muscles of the weight-bearing foot.

1 Stand up straight with your body well balanced – head up, shoulders down, back and relaxed, bottom tucked neatly under, tummy in. Slowly raise your left leg, bend your knee and turn it outwards. Then take your foot and tuck it into the top of the inside of your right thigh. When you have found your balance raise your arms above your head and place the palms of your hands together in true Yogi style. Hold for a moment, then change legs.

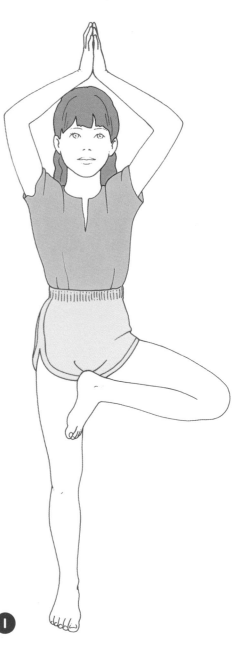

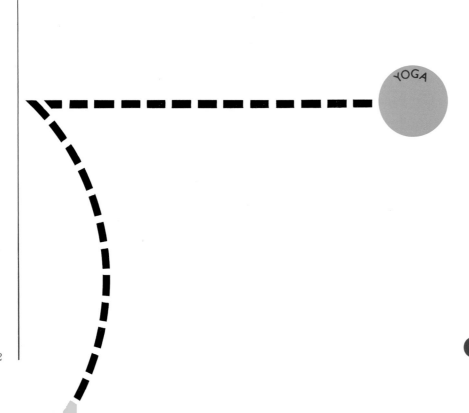

YOGA

FROG BALANCE

FOR ADULTS, AND CHILDREN FROM SEVEN YEARS.

Aim: tones and strengthens tummy, arms and shoulder muscles. Helps develop balance.

This exercise is as hard as it looks. Don't worry if you can't manage to do it at first. Place cushions round you in case you topple over.

1 Squat on the floor with your legs apart, hands flat and comfortably on the floor in front of you, between your legs.

2 Bend your elbows slightly and push them gently against the insides of your knees. Slowly lean forward, taking all your weight onto your hands and arms. If you find this hard, support yourself by leaving some of your weight on your toes.

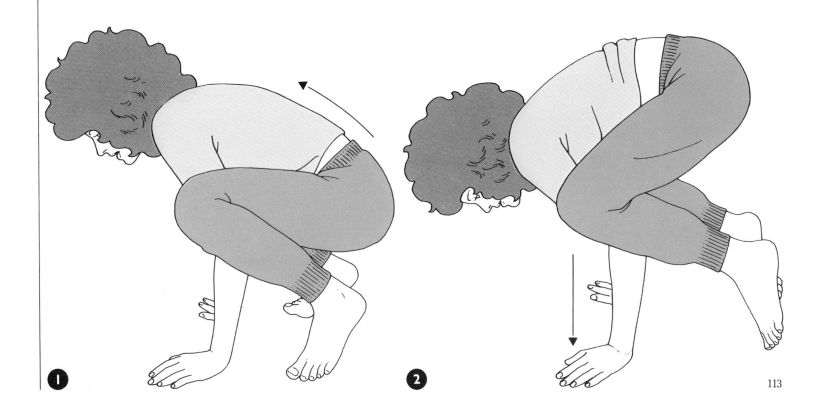

1

2

113

T-TIME

FOR ADULTS, AND CHILDREN FROM FOUR YEARS.

Aim: improves balance and strengthens muscles of the back, legs and feet.

Make the shape of a capital 'T' with your body. The leg you stand on is the downwards stroke of the 'T', the rest of your body is stretched out horizontally to make the cross bar.

1 Stand up straight with your legs together. Stretch your arms out in front of you at shoulder level and, balancing on your right leg, slowly raise your left leg behind you.

2 Keeping your back straight raise your left leg straight out behind you. Keep your arms stretched out in front of you.

3 Lean forwards and bring your left leg back up and out so that your whole body from the tip of your hands to your left toe is in as straight a line as possible. Try to keep your supporting leg as straight as you can, but don't worry if you can't at first. See who can make the best letter 'T'.

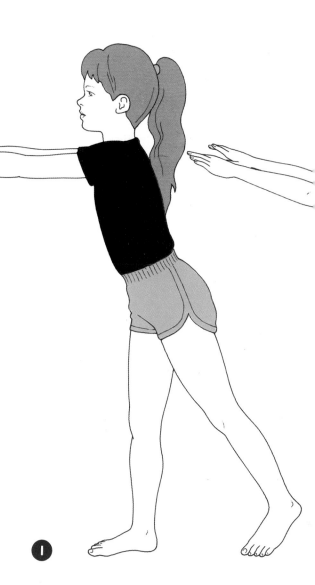

INTRODUCTION

Cooling down your body after vigorous exercise is just as important as warming it up beforehand. Suddenly stopping moving can put a strain on the heart as it has to work extra hard to cope with all the blood that is being rushed to it from the muscles for fresh oxygen. Gentle exercise slowly returns your heartbeat and breathing to normal. This is why athletes always jog after a race, however tired they are.

RELAXABEND

FOR ADULTS, AND CHILDREN FROM EIGHTEEN MONTHS.

Aim: relaxes the body and stretches the spine out after a strenuous bout of exercise games.

You'll feel a gentle pull all the way up your spine as you curve your body over your knees and rest your head on the floor.

1 Kneel on the floor and sit back on your feet, back straight and arms relaxed by your sides.

2 Keeping your bottom on your feet, bend your body forward so that your tummy rests on your thighs and your head rests on the floor. Let your arms lie loosely beside you. Relax like this for a minute.

RAG DOLLS

FOR ADULTS, AND CHILDREN FROM THREE YEARS.

Aim: cools down the body by relaxing it bit by bit.

Pretend you are a rag doll propped up straight and gradually go floppy and loose, starting from your head and working down.

1 Stand up straight but relaxed, arms by your sides, legs comfortably apart and eyes wide open.

2 Starting from the top of your body, slowly relax and go floppy. First your head and neck, then shoulders. Feel them go heavy and limp.

1

2

3 Slowly, vertebrae by vertebrae, allow your body to droop forward until you are bending from the waist, hands dangling loosely towards the ground. Only bend down as far as you can comfortably lift yourself up without straining.

4 Now slowly bring yourself back up again. Unfold your spine from your waist upwards, returning to a standing position as you put life back into your body.

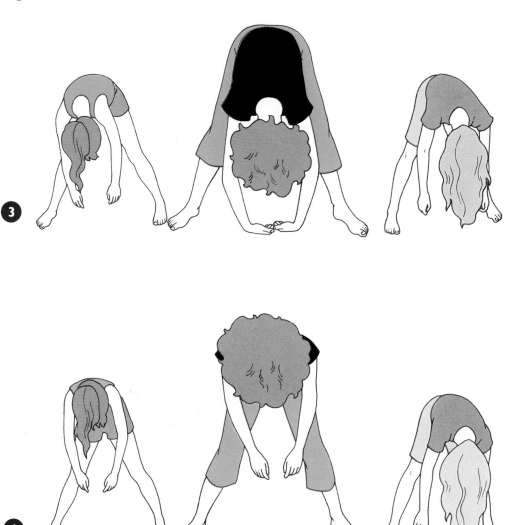

MUSLIM PRAYER STRETCH

FOR ADULTS, AND CHILDREN FROM EIGHTEEN MONTHS.

Aim: stretches and relaxes the body.

Muslims pray many times each day. They kneel on the floor with their arms stretched out in front of them. It is very relaxing.

1 Kneel on all fours and, moving your hands as little as possible, lower your bottom onto your feet. Keep your arms stretched out in front of you and relax in this position with your forehead resting on the floor.

2 Now stretch your body by slowly walking your fingers forwards a few centimetres. Relax a moment then walk them out a little further. Relax again then walk them out as far as you can.

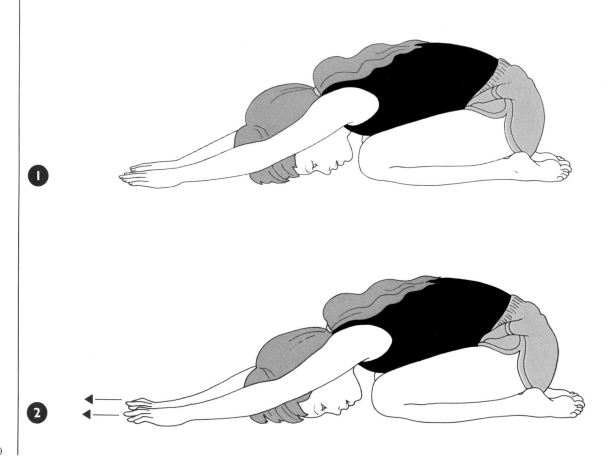

120

MARBLE ARCH

FOR ADULTS, AND CHILDREN FROM EIGHTEEN MONTHS.

Aim: stretches the spine to help make it more supple and helps to relax you.

Don't do this cool-down exercise if you have any back problems because it works the lower back muscles that are easily strained.

1 Lie on your back with your arms at your sides, legs together and relaxed.

2 Slowly tense your body as you clench your hands into fists, push them against the floor and arch your back, pushing up your chest and tilting your head back slightly. Hold this position as you count to two, then slowly relax and carefully let your body subside back to the starting position, letting your head slide back.

1

2

121

DEAD LIONS

COOL DOWN

FOR ADULTS, AND CHILDREN FROM EIGHTEEN MONTHS.

Aim: relaxes the body and gives a good supported twist to the spine. Gently stretches and lengthens the body so it can breathe freely and deeply.

1 Lie on your back with your arms stretched out to either side. Bend your knees up to your chest and then relax and drop them as far as they will go over to the left. Then turn your head to the right and relax in this position for three minutes. Repeat, dropping your legs over to the right and turning your head to the left.

2 Stay in this position for a minute then move your legs to the right of your body and your head to the left.

1

SLEEPING BEAUTY

FOR ADULTS, AND CHILDREN FROM EIGHTEEN MONTHS.

Aim: relaxes and cools down the body after a lively bout of exercise games.

① Be a sleeping beauty. Pretend you are under a spell which keeps you in a deep, deep, sleep. Lie on your back and relax your whole body. Keep your eyes closed and let yourself go all floaty. When a few hundred years have gone by, a handsome prince will ride by and wake you with a kiss, waking you from your dreams.

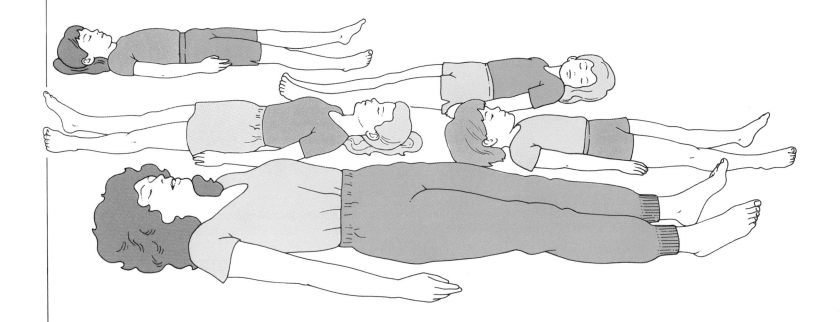

①

PHYSICAL MILESTONES

This is a rough guide to the physical skills you can expect your child to master as he/she grows in strength and dexterity. But don't expect all children to follow this pattern exactly; children vary hugely and it is quite normal for some to be able to do some things earlier, or a few months later, than in the list below.

ONE YEAR
1. Can sit up from lying position without pulling up on anything.
2. Pulls to stand, and walks sideways around furniture.
3. May stand alone for a moment.
4. Usually able to walk with one hand held, or may take a few steps alone.
5. Fine pincer grip (i.e. can pick up small objects such as peas).
6. Points with index finger.

FIFTEEN MONTHS
1. Kneels on floor without support.
2. Can crawl upstairs on hands and knees.
3. Can get from lying on tummy to standing up unaided.
4. Stands alone for several seconds.
5. Can usually take a few steps alone, starting and stopping him/herself.
6. Pincer grip more precise (i.e. can pick up crumbs rather than peas).
7. Can make lines with a crayon, but held with whole hand.
8. Can grasp two cubes in one hand.
9. Builds tower of two-brick height (after demonstration).
10. Can take off shoes.

EIGHTEEN MONTHS
1. Walks well, seldom falling; stops and starts safely.
2. Can push or pull large toys across floor, or walk with a pull-along toy.
3. Can carry a toy while walking around.
4. Can lower to squatting position to pick up toy.
5. Climbs up stairs with aid of banisters or supporting hand.
6. Enjoys scribbling; uses whole hand and sometimes thumb and middle finger grasp.
7. Turns pages of book, often several at a time.
8. Can build a three-cube tower (after demonstration).
9. Can take off socks and gloves.

TWO YEARS
1. Runs steadily, stopping and starting at will.
2. Climbs furniture.
3. Walks backwards.
4. Squats to play.
5. Climbs stairs with two feet per step, holding onto rail.
6. Sits astride scooter-type toys and pushes with feet on floor.
7. Throws a ball without overbalancing.
8. Can turn single pages of a book.
9. Can build a six-to-seven-cube tower.
10. Beginning to dress his/herself.
11. Turns doorknobs, and unscrews lids.
12. Scribbles are now circular; can imitate a vertical stroke.
13. Hand preference usually shown (i.e. right/left handed).

TWO AND A HALF YEARS
1. Can jump with both feet from a low step.
2. Can stand on tiptoe (after demonstration).
3. Able to kick a ball, but inaccurately.
4. Can hold pencil between thumb and middle finger.

THREE YEARS

1. Walking and running are now quite mature.
2. Can stand on one foot, unaided, for a few seconds.
3. Climbs up stairs with one foot per step; climbs down with two feet per step.
4. Kicks ball easily.
5. Can pedal a tricycle steering around corners.
6. Can thread large beads.
7. Can unbutton large buttons.
8. Can cut with scissors.
9. Washes and dries hands.
10. Can imitate crudely a drawing of a cross.

FOUR YEARS

1. Can climb up and down stairs like an adult, one foot per step.
2. Can hop on dominant foot (i.e. preferred foot).
3. Can catch, throw and kick a ball.
4. Can build a bridge with three bricks.
5. Can thread fine beads using stiff thread or a needle.
6. Can copy circles and crosses.

FIVE YEARS

1. Can walk along a narrow line.
2. Can hop forwards on either foot.
3. Can move or march to rhythm.
4. Skips
5. Stands on one foot for 10 seconds.
6. Skilled on a climbing frame and swing.
7. Beginning to write; good control of pen or brush.
8. Can draw a recognisable human figure.
9. Colours neatly.

PACKED LUNCHES

It can be difficult to keep coming up with fresh ideas for packed lunches which are both good for your children and tasty. Take inspiration from the following suggestions and think up more of your own, but don't think of packed lunches just in terms of sandwiches: if you invest in small airtight plastic containers and plastic spoons the variety of foods you can prepare are endless.

For a well-balanced packed lunch always choose something from each of the following three groups . . .

Potato, bread, rice, pasta, beans.

Salad, vegetables and/or fresh fruit.

Meat, fish, nut butter, bean spread (hummus).

- Chicken joint, chopped cold potato, tomato and cucumber wedges, fruit yogurt (natural yogurt and fruit purée in a sealed container).
- Salad of tuna fish (well drained), cucumber, baked beans or red kidney beans, sweetcorn, cold pasta plus a wholemeal roll. Rock cake.
- Peanut butter sandwiches without extra butter or margarine on the bread. Banana.
- Hummus with bread fingers, sticks of cucumber and carrot to dip into it. Packet of nuts and raisins, peeled orange.
- Egg and tomato sandwiches (hard boil an egg and add chopped tomato mixed with a little yogurt and tomato purée to moisten it so you don't need butter or margarine. Spread it straight onto the bread). Apple and digestive biscuit.
- Piece of cold quiche (pastry filled with egg, milk, peas and other veg.). Brown rice plus sweetcorn, apple and cucumber. Melon wedge.

SNACKS AND NIBBLES

Stave off hunger pangs in between meals by nibbling one of the following healthy snacks.

- Pumpkin, sunflower or melon seeds.
- Nuts and raisins.
- Plain biscuits topped with cottage cheese and pineapple or chives.
- Dried apricots
- Fresh bread roll or a piece of fruit or raw carrot or stick of celery.
- Plain yogurt and fruit/fruit purée.
- Breadsticks

USEFUL ADDRESSES

BRITISH DENTAL HEALTH FOUNDATION
Kingston House,
7 London Road,
Old Strafford,
Bucks RG12 5BY

CHISWICK FAMILY RESCUE
369 Chiswick High Road,
London W4
01 747 0133

CONTACT A FAMILY (for parents of
mentally and/or physically handicapped
children)
(Registered charity)
16 Strutton Ground,
London SW1
01 222 2695

CRUSE (The National Organisation for the
Widowed and their Children),
Cruse House,
126 Sheen Road,
Richmond,
Surrey TW9 1UR
01 940 4818 or 9047

EQUAL PAY AND OPPORTUNITY
CAMPAIGN
45 College Cross,
London N1

FAMILY FORUM
Cambridge House,
131 Camberwell Road,
London SE5
01 703 8706/6413

GINGERBREAD
25 Wellington Street,
London WC2 E7BN
01 240 0953

GIRL GUIDES ASSOCIATION
17-19 Buckingham Palace Road
London SW1 W0PT
01 834 6242

HANDICAPPED ADVENTURE
PLAYGROUND ASSOCIATION
Fulham Palace,
Bishops Park,
London SW6.
01 736 4443

KEEP FIT ASSOCIATION
16 Upper Woburn Place,
London WC1H 0QG
01 387 4349

MATERNITY ALLIANCE
59-61 Camden High Street,
London NW1 7JL
01 388 6337

NATIONAL ADVISORY CENTRE
ON CAREERS FOR WOMEN
Drayton House,
30 Gordon Street,
London WC1H 0AX
01 380 0117

NATIONAL ASSOCIATION FOR THE
WELFARE OF CHILDREN IN HOSPITAL
(NAWCH), Argyle House,
29-31 Euston Road,
London NW1 2SD
01 833 2041

NATIONAL CHILDBIRTH TRUST
9 Queensborough Terrace,
London W2 3TB
01 221 3833

PRE-SCHOOL PLAYGROUPS
ASSOCIATION
Alford House,
Aveline Street,
London SE11 5DH
01 582 8871